From Norfolk Knobs to Fidget Pie

Traditional foods from the Midlands and East Anglia

From Norfolk Knobs to Fidget Pie

Traditional foods from the Midlands and East Anglia

Laura Mason and Catherine Brown
Foreword by Hugh Fearnley-Whittingstall

HarperPress
An imprint of HarperCollinsPublishers

Harper*Press*
An imprint of HarperCollins*Publishers*
77–85 Fulham Palace Road
Hammersmith, London W6 8JB
www.harpercollins.co.uk

Published by Harper Press in 2007

First published in Great Britain in 1999
as part of *Traditional Foods of Britain*
by Prospect Books
Allaleigh House, Blackawton, Totnes, Devon TQ9 7DL
Copyright © 1999, 2004, edition and arrangement, Prospect Books
Copyright © 1999, text, GEIE/Euroterroirs, Paris

Subsequently published by Harper*Press* in 2006 as part of *The Taste of Britain*
Original design by 'OMEDESIGN
Copyright © 2007, edition and arrangement, Harper*Press*
Copyright © 2007, Foreword, Hugh Fearnley-Whittingstall
Copyright © 2007, Preface, Laura Mason and Catherine Brown
Copyright © contributions on p.14/28-9/57/91; individual authors
(see Acknowledgements)

This edition produced for The Book People Ltd.,
Hall Wood Avenue, Haydock, St. Helens, WA11 9UL.

9 8 7 6 5 4 3 2 1

A catalogue record for this book
is available from the British Library

ISBN: 978-0-00-779-841-4

Design by Envy Design Ltd

Printed and bound in China

From Norfolk Knobs to Fidget Pie is part of a series of books about regional British food which include:

From Bath Chaps to Bara Brith
The Taste of South West Britain

Bedfordshire Clangers and Lardy Cake
Traditional Foods from the South and South East

From Eccles Cake to Hawkshead Wig
A Celebration of Northern Food

From Petticoat Tails to Arbroath Smokies
Traditional Foods of Scotland

These books originally formed part of the complete volume, *The Taste of Britain*, published by HarperPress in 2006.

Contents

Foreword

Much is made these days of British food culture. Chefs and food writers, myself included, are keen to tell you that it's thriving, it should be celebrated, it's as good as anything our Continental cousins enjoy. Yet sometimes it seems as if our words come rolling back to us, as if bouncing off some distant landmass, unheard and unheeded along the way, so that we begin to have trouble persuading ourselves, let alone others, that there is something here worth fighting for.

The fact is that if you spend much time in supermarkets, or amongst the proliferation of branded fast foods on any high street, or if you eat in any but a handful of UK restaurants or pubs, then the concept of regional British food can seem a bit like Father Christmas, or Nirvana. A lovely romantic idea, but it doesn't really exist, does it?

Well, yes, it does. And if you're having trouble finding it, it may just be because you are looking in the wrong place. The problem, in part at least, is that the best, most uplifting stories about British food culture are being drowned out by the cacophony of mediocrity, and worse. The Turkey Twizzler is front page news – and rightly so, when it is making pre-basted, additive-laced butterballs of our children themselves. Shavings of Turkey 'ham' – 98 per cent fat free, of course – are filling the sandwiches of figure-conscious office workers the length and breadth of the nation. But the Norfolk Black, a real turkey slow-grown and bred for flavour, is out there, too – waiting to show you what he's worth. He's not making a song and dance – just gobbling quietly to himself. Track him down, and you're in for a revelation.

That's why this series of books are so timely, so necessary – and so brilliantly useful. They are a map, an investigative tool that will enable you to leave behind the homogenous and the bland, and set off on an exciting journey to find Britain's edible treasure – some of which may turn out to be hidden on your very doorstep.

I urge you not merely to browse them, but to use them. Because if you can get out there and discover for yourself some of our great British specialities – whether it's traditional sage Derby cheese, or the Yorkshire teacakes known as Fat Rascals, or a properly aged Suffolk cider vinegar – then you will discover, or at least remind yourself, that food can be so much more than fuel. That it can, several times a day, every day of our lives, relax us, stimulate us, and give us pleasure.

The foods described in this book can all work that small daily miracle of exciting our passions. Not all of them, for all of us. But each of them for some of us. They have been made and honed over generations – sometimes centuries – and they are still with us because enough of us – sometimes only just enough of us – love them. Of course, in many instances, we have yet to discover whether we love them or not. And that is why this book is so loaded with fantastic potential. Everybody has a new favourite food waiting for them in the pages ahead.

I've travelled fairly widely, if somewhat randomly, around Britain, and tracking down and tasting local foods has become an increasing priority for me. Very uplifting it is, too. Approach our regional food culture with a true sense of curiosity, and you can never become an old hand, or a jaded palate. I still feel a great sense of excitement and discovery when I finally get to eat a classic local dish on its own home turf. You can't easily deconstruct the magic formula of a well-made Lancashire Hot Pot, or a Dorset apple cake. It is in the nature of such dishes that their sum is greater than their parts. But you can, when you find a version that hits the spot, instantly appreciate how such dishes have survived the harsh natural selection of public taste, and come to delight, comfort and sustain families and groups of friends for so long.

Recently, for instance, I managed to track down my very first proper Yorkshire curd tart, its delectable filling made from colostrum – the very rich milk produced by a cow for her newborn calf. It was baked for me by a farmer's wife at home in her own kitchen, using the method passed down to her through her family, and it was wonderful – very rich, curdy and slightly crumbly – having a hint of cakiness without the flouriness (I told you deconstruction was a vain enterprise). Anyway, it was a world away from any 'regular' custard tart I'd tried before. What I learnt from that experience, and from many similar ones, is that regionality really does matter. If that tart had been made in Dorset or in the Highlands, it wouldn't have tasted the same. And if it had not been made at all, the world – and on that drizzly autumn day, me – would have been the poorer for it.

There are so many factors that affect the way a food turns out. Cheese is the best example. I love cheese – 'milk's leap toward immortality' as someone once said – and it never ceases to amaze me. It's made from milk, of course, plus something that will make the milk curdle (usually rennet, but sometimes quirkier coagulants, like nettle juice). Two basic ingredients. Yet cheese is one of the most diverse foods known to man. There are hundreds of varieties in the British Isles alone – and a bowlful of fresh, pillowy Scottish crowdie differs so greatly from a nutty Somerset cheddar that it's hard to believe they're basically the same stuff. The breed of cattle and their diet, the local water and pasture, the yeasts and bacteria that live locally in the air, the techniques used to curdle the milk, the way the cheese is pressed, turned, and aged – all these things affect the outcome.

That's why it seems absolutely right to me that only cheese made in a handful of Midlands dairies can be called Stilton, and that beer brewed with the gypsum-rich water in Burton-upon-Trent is labelled as such. What's more, if you understand why regional products are unique – that it's high temperatures and seaweed fertiliser that make Jersey Royals taste different to any other potatoes, for instance – then you know more about food in general. An understanding of regional diversity can only make us more intelligent and appreciative eaters.

This understanding is not always easy to come by. Most other European countries have long taken for granted that local foods should be protected, their unique identity preserved. Hence the French

AOC and the Italian DOC systems. But it's an idea not everyone in this country is comfortable with. I put this down to two things, and the first is the creeping curse of supermarket culture. The big multiple retailers try to tell us that we can eat whatever we want, whenever we want and indeed wherever we want. If you understand the seasonal nature of fresh produce, you know this is neither true nor desirable – and the same goes for regionality. You might not be able to buy genuine Arbroath smokies in every shop in the land, but that is precisely what makes them special when you do find them.

The second reason for resistance to regional labelling is illustrated by the pork pie issue. The pie makers of Melton Mowbray are currently battling to have their product awarded PGI (Protected Geographic Indication) status. That would mean only pies made in the area, to a traditional recipe, could carry the name. Other pork pie makers, from other areas, object to this. They want to call their products Melton Mowbray pies, too, arguing that their recipe is much the same. That's nonsense, of course: a recipe is only the beginning of a dish, a mere framework. The where, the how and the who of its making are just as important. But why would you even want to call your pie a Mowbray pie if it comes from London, or Swansea? Only, perhaps, if you know the real Mowbray pies taste better, and you can't be bothered to make your own recipe good enough to compete.

All of which goes to show why the issue of regionality is as relevant today as it ever has been. It's important not to see *From Norfolk Knobs to Fidget Pie* as a history book, a compendium of nostalgic culinary whimsy. The food included here is alive and well, and there is nothing described in these pages that you can't eat today, as long as you go to the right place. That's perhaps the most important criterion for inclusion because our regional food traditions are just as much part of the future as the past. At least, they had better be, or we will be in serious trouble.

The implications for our health, and the health of our environment, are far-reaching. If we eat, say, fruit that's produced locally, not only do we reduce the food miles that are wrecking our climate, but that fruit will be fresher and richer in nutrients. If we can go to a butcher's shop to buy meat that's been raised nearby, we can ask the butcher how it was farmed, and how it was slaughtered. And perhaps we can take our children with us, so they learn something too. In the end, a local food culture, supplied in the main by contiguous communities, militates against secrecy, adulteration – cruelty even – and in favour of transparency, accountability and good practice. What could be more reassuring than knowing the names and addresses of the people who produce your food?

I don't think it's overstating the case, either, to say that a knowledge of regional cooking promotes resourcefulness and a renewed respect for food in all of us. Regional dishes are, by their very nature, simple things. This is folk cooking – a 'nose to tail' approach that uses whatever's available and makes it go as far as possible. For a while now – since conspicuous consumption has become practically an end in itself – our predecessors' abhorrence of throwing away anything may have seemed at best, quaint, at worst, laughable. But as we begin to come to terms with the consequences of our 'have it all now' culture, it is becoming clear that ethical production, good husbandry, environmental responsibility and kitchen thrift all go hand in hand. The frugal culture that gave birth to chitterlings and lardy cake, Bath chaps and bread pudding is something we should be proud to belong to. To re-embrace it can only do us good.

Aside from their currency, the foods in this book have had to prove themselves in other ways. They must be unique to a specific region and they must have longevity, having been made or produced for at least 75 years. Finally, they must be, to use a rather ugly word, 'artisanal'. That means that special knowledge and skills are required to make them properly. Which brings me to one crucial element of good food that should never be forgotten: the people who make it. Almost without exception, the brewers, bakers, cooks, farmers and fishermen who produce traditional foods are what you might call 'characters'. This doesn't mean they are yokels caught in a yesteryear time warp. They are people of passion and commitment, intelligence and good humour, and often extraordinary specialist knowledge. And they know more than most of us about the meaning of life.

Not a single one of them goes to work in the morning in order to make lots of money – you certainly don't choose to devote your life to bannock-making in the hope it will furnish you with a swimming pool and a Ferrari. They do it because they believe in it and, ultimately, feel it is worthwhile. In their own quiet and industrious way, they understand just how much is at stake. The future of civilized, communal, respectful life on our islands? It is not preposterous to suggest it. Use your regular custom and generously expressed enthusiasm to support this modest army of dedicated souls, working away in their kitchens, gardens, orchards breweries and smokehouses all over Britain, and you do a great deal more than simply save a cheese, or a beer, for posterity. You help save the next generation from the tyranny of industrial mediocrity.

Amid this talk of pride and principles, it's crucial not to lose sight of the fact that this is food to be enjoyed, celebrated – and shared with friends. Dishes don't survive down the centuries unless they taste good. You may not need much persuasion to try some of the buttery cakes or fabulously fresh fruit and veg described in these pages. But you will perhaps need a sense of adventure to rediscover the charms of some of the entries. Be ready to cast your squeamishness aside and sample some tripe, some tongue, some trotters as well. If the experience of visitors to our River Cottage events here in Dorset is anything to go by, I'm betting you'll be pleasantly surprised. You'll be taking a pig's head home from the butcher's and making your own brawn before you can say, 'Er, not for me, thanks.'

One element of this series of books to be richly savoured is the language. They are written, by Laura Mason and Catherine Brown, without hyperbole, but with a precision and clarity that far better express their authors' underlying passion and purpose. Another thing that makes them a joy to read is their embrace of the regional food vernacular: Dorset knobs, Puggie Buns, Singin' Hinnnies, Black Bullets and Mendip Wallfish are all to be revelled in for their names alone. Indeed, some might be tempted to enjoy them chiefly as a glorious catalogue of eccentricity, a celebration of the cowsheel and the careless gooseberry, of the head cheese and the damson cheese (neither of which are actually cheese) that make British food so charming and idiosyncratic.

But to do so would be to miss out. Now that this book exists, now that it is in your hands, use it to bring about change. It should not be taken as a slice of the past, in aspic, but as a well-stocked store cupboard, with the potential to enrich our future food culture. See it not as a preservation order for British regional foods, but a call to action. Use this book as a guide, not merely to seek out delicious things that you've never tried before, but also to recreate some of them in your own kitchen. Do that and you'll be actively participating in a great food culture that has always been with us, that is often hidden beneath the mass-produced, homogenous, seasonless food we are so frequently offered, but which may yet have a vibrant future.

This book - along with the rest in the series - is a thorough and splendid answer to the question 'What is British food?' Use it well, and it may help to ensure that is still a meaningful question a hundred years from now.

Hugh Fearnley-Whittingstall

Preface

In 1994 we embarked on a mission to describe as many British foods with regional affiliations as we could find. We were part of a Europe-wide project working within a framework – handed down from Brussels – which demanded a link to the *terroir* (soil). In fact the project, named Euroterroir, was more suited to rural southern Europe than industrialized, urbanized Britain. How do you link Yorkshire Relish to the soil? But ultimately we succeeded in writing up some four hundred British entries. And along the way we asked some broader questions – what are our traditional foods? What is the character of British taste?

We've discovered that many rural treasures had survived against the odds. That sometimes foods with traditional or regional affiliations languished unloved. That sometimes British foods, though not always linking directly to the *terroir*, did have other powerful historical influences which made them special, and distinct, from the rest of Europe. No other country in Europe has a history of spicing to match the British.

Yet our homogenized food supply was clearly inflicting a far-reaching loss of local distinctiveness and quality. The idea, inherent in the project, that foods should be the property of a place and its community (*terroir*, in the context of food in France, carries implications of regionality, cultural groupings and the influence of trade and climate), rather than the trademarked possession of an individual or company, was especially alien.

Our initial research complete, we felt confident that either the Ministry of Agriculture or Food from Britain would take up the cause and publish a book based on the work which had taken us two years to complete. Instead, it was a small publisher in Devon (Tom Jaine of

Prospect Books) who kept the flag flying and *Traditional Foods of Britain* was published in 1999. Eight years on, we welcome this series published by HarperCollins.

We also welcome signs of change. Now, there is more awareness of commercial dilution, and dishonest imitation and therefore the need to protect food names, though the application process for producers is slow and difficult. There are certainly more small producers working locally, but they have to cope with numerous barriers. However much they protest otherwise, powerful supermarket central distribution systems and cut-throat pricing polices are not designed to foster local produce. And consumers do not always pause to consider the more subtle and elusive nuances of foods from closer to home.

Of course the ties of regionality do not suit foodstuffs, and in any case should be just one of many avenues open to British farmers and food producers. But it would be good to see more raw local ingredients transformed into distinctive foods since records show their rich variety in the past. Shops and markets bursting with colourful and varied local produce are one of the great pleasures of shopping for food on the continent. They exist because national policies and local custom support them. They should not be impossible in Britain. These books are not an end, but a beginning.

Laura Mason and Catherine Brown 2007

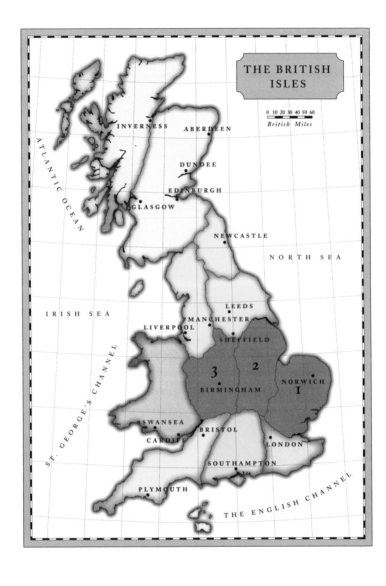

THE BRITISH
ISLES

0 10 20 30 40 50 60
British Miles

ATLANTIC OCEAN

INVERNESS   ABERDEEN

DUNDEE

EDINBURGH

GLASGOW

NEWCASTLE

NORTH SEA

IRISH SEA

LEEDS

MANCHESTER

LIVERPOOL

SHEFFIELD

3   2

BIRMINGHAM   NORWICH
                    1

ST. GEORGE'S CHANNEL

SWANSEA

CARDIFF   BRISTOL

LONDON

SOUTHAMPTON

PLYMOUTH

THE ENGLISH CHANNEL

Regions

1. *East Anglia*

2. *East Midlands*

3. *West Midlands*

East Anglia

Bramley's Seedling Apple

DESCRIPTION:

A LATE-SEASON COOKING APPLE, DESCRIBED BY MORGAN & RICHARDS (1993) AS LARGE TO VERY LARGE (OVER 7.5–8CM DIAMETER), THE SHAPE FLAT-ROUND, OFTEN LOPSIDED, WITH A BROAD BASIN OF MEDIUM DEPTH, WHICH IS RIBBED AND PUCKERED; THE EYE LARGE, CLOSED OR PARTIALLY OPEN; THE SEPALS BROAD AND DOWNY; THE CAVITY QUITE BROAD AND DEEP, LINED WITH RUSSET, AND THE STALK SHORT AND THICK; THE COLOUR OF THE SKIN CHARACTERISTICALLY GREEN OR GREENISH YELLOW, WITH BROWNISH ORANGE FLUSH, BROAD RED STRIPES AND LENTICELS AS RUSSET DOTS; THE FLESH WHITE TINGED WITH GREEN; THE FLAVOUR IS ACID, WITH A SHARP APPLE TASTE RETAINED EVEN WHEN COOKED AND SWEETENED.

HISTORY:

In Britain, apples are divided into those used for dessert and those used for cooking. Bramley's Seedling is the foremost example of the latter. The original was raised in the early nineteenth century by Mary Anne Brailsford in Nottinghamshire. The tree attracted attention in the 1850s, and was commercialized thereafter. It remains very important and can only be grown successfully in Britain. It is an apple of the type known as a codlin. Originally this seems to have denoted an immature apple, unsuitable for eating raw; this was the sense the word carried in the seventeenth century (*OED*). Later, it had come to mean a hard apple intended for coddling or cooking. A characteristic of these is that they collapse in a froth when cooked.

These cooking apples were very much to British taste and British climate. The Bramley displaced the earlier Victorian favourite, Dumelow's Seedling. This last was the apple that may have sired

Newton Wonder, a famous breed that was first located as a seedling growing in the thatch of a Derbyshire inn – considered by some to be a cross of Blenheim Orange and Dumelow's. A further cross-breeding, early last century, between Newton Wonder and Blenheim Orange was the start of an apple called Howgate Wonder. Both this and the Newgate Wonder are still sometimes found on sale. All these breeds are old-fashioned codlins of the British sort.

Bramleys were first cultivated on a large scale in the 1880s, particularly in East Anglia – above all around Wisbech (Cambridgeshire) where orchards of tall old trees underplanted with gooseberries survived until the 1980s, although now much diminished in area. This pattern of planting is very old, 'similar to that advised by Austen in 1657' (Roach, 1985).

Bramley apples are much used by the food processing industry for sauces, purées and pie fillings; for juicing, when they are usually included in blends; and also as part of blends for cider, especially in East Anglia.

TECHNIQUE:

Since the 1920s, rootstocks for grafting apple trees have been standardized in Britain, using stock developed at East Malling Research Station in Kent, a major centre of apple growing. Dwarf stock is now favoured. Intensive modern orchards now grow about 3,000 trees per hectare, renewed every 10–15 years. In old orchards, it was about 110 per hectare, renewed every 50 years, but few of these now survive. The trees are trained into a pyramid, with low horizontal branches bearing the burden of crop. The old orchards planted in the Wisbech area used vigorous M12 or M13 rootstocks, planted 13 metres square, inteplanted with gooseberries. Bramleys are a fairly hardy variety, relatively tolerant of a wide range of soils. Optimum pollination time is early to mid-May, and the variety is partly triploid, requiring 2 pollinators (Worcester Pearmain is a variety used for this); it is a heavy cropper, but prone to bitter pit. For commercial apple production, the fruit is chemically analysed to determine storage potential; picking is then carried out by hand. Bramleys are picked in early October. Grading is by diameter (sizes are set according to variety) and by quality (EU standards, for appearance) into Grade 1 or Grade 2. Storage is in controlled atmosphere (low in oxygen, high in carbon dioxide) and temperature. Bramleys have benefited greatly from the development of controlled-atmosphere storage techniques, which now allow for 10 months' storage.

REGION OF PRODUCTION:
EAST ANGLIA.

Cambridge Gage

DESCRIPTION:

A SMALL-MEDIUM ROUND PLUM, WITH FLESH THAT CLINGS TO THE STONE. COLOUR: MOST GAGES ARE GREEN RIPENING TO AMBER; TRANSPARENT GAGES HAVE SEMI-TRANSPARENT SKINS. FLAVOUR: JUICY TENDER FLESH, WITH WELL-BALANCED SHARP-SWEET FLAVOUR.

HISTORY:

The plum has had a long history in Britain. The sloe (*Prunus spinosa*) is found in the wild; there have been archaeological finds of bullace (*Prunus institia*) stones – the antecedent of the damson; and the domestic plum (*Prunus domestica*), which is a hybridization of the wild cherry plum or Myrobalan and the sloe, seems also to have existed in Roman Britain (Roach, 1985). Further varieties were known and cultivated in the Middle Ages and improved breeds were encouraged and imported during the Tudor and Stuart period. Among these were plums of the Reine Claude group, so called after its introduction into France from Italy in the reign of François I (d. 1547). This type was described by writers in England during the seventeenth century. They were probably known earlier, as their stones were found in the wreck of the *Mary Rose*, which sank off Southampton in 1545. If the French called this 'sweet, tender and juicy' (Roach, 1985) variety after their Queen, the English took even longer to think up a name. Some time before 1724, plum trees of the Reine Claude type were sent to Sir Thomas Gage at Hengrave Hall in Suffolk from his brother who was a Catholic priest in France. The saplings lost their labels in transit and Sir Thomas's gardener simply called them 'Green Gages'. Not much time was lost before they were being listed under this name by London nurserymen. The garden writer Philip Miller described them in 1731 as 'one of the best plums in England'.

Most high-quality English plum varieties were of foreign origin until the end of George III's reign. One East Anglian cultivar, the Fotheringham, is mentioned in 1665, and the Bury St Edmunds (Suffolk) gardener, Jervaise Coe, developed Coe's Golden Drop at the end of the eighteenth century. The real work of breeding and expansion of the English plum list was by Thomas Rivers, a nurseryman working in East Anglia in the years after 1834.

The plum is a fruit that often produces chance seedlings that prove to be of great worth. They are almost invariably propagated by suckers taken from the original *trouvaille*, and they are usually taken up by farmers, gardeners and growers in the district immediately local to their discovery. Kea plums (Cornwall), Purple Pershore (Worcestershire) and Dittisham plums (Devon) are examples of this process. Another was the Cambridge Gage. Its origin is unknown, but it is indubitably a seedling of a Green Gage (Smith, 1978), though showing 'greater vigour and better cropping'. It is grown much around Cambridge, was received at the National Fruit Trials in 1927, and was thought 'the best of all the old English gages' by the gourmet André Simon (1960).

TECHNIQUE:

Cambridge Gages form large, vigorous trees, but these can be kept relatively compact by appropriate pruning in summer. For large-scale commercial growing, St Julien A is the favoured rootstock. This makes an earlier-cropping and smaller tree than some. Cambridge Gages are self-pollinating under good conditions, but ideally a pollinator of another mid-season flowering plum variety should be planted close by. The variety is less demanding than some gages, fairly hardy and resistant to pests and diseases, but the fruit has a tendency to split if there is heavy rainfall at the point of ripening. It is also an erratic cropper. Nevertheless, the flavour is considered so good that one company, Wilkin of Tiptree in Essex, use only this variety for greengage-based preserves and jams.

REGION OF PRODUCTION:
EAST ANGLIA.

Careless Gooseberry

DESCRIPTION:
CARELESS HAS LARGE, YELLOW, SLIGHTLY SWEET FRUIT USED FOR COOKING.

HISTORY:

The gooseberry, *Ribes grossularia*, a plant native to Europe, has been cultivated since at least the fifteenth century in Britain. It is a very popular fruit in early summer. It has been used in a tradition of cooked, sweetened desserts which extends back at least to the early seventeenth century. These include gooseberry fool, pies and tarts, all important today. 'One of the servants partook too plentifully last night of gooseberry-fool after a rout his lordship gave … and she is dead this morning of cholera morbus,' quipped George Augustus Sala (1859), reflecting the perennial attraction of the fruit. The bush is easy to cultivate and takes up little space. It was much grown by poor people and many gardens and allotments contain at least one example.

The earliest cultivated varieties that receive literary and botanical notice seem to have been imported into this country during the sixteenth century from Flanders and northern Germany, where it was also much valued. In France, and countries further south, it was little esteemed, or even known. The French called it *groseille à maquereau*, recognizing its cardinal virtue as a sauce for mackerel (appreciated in the province of Normandy). The English, too, may have called it after its culinary use – the berry to be served as sauce for goose. The name was not at all fixed throughout the nation – there were alternative names of feaberry (North Country), feabes (pronounced fapes, in Norfolk), carberry and wineberry.

During the eighteenth century, a custom of competitive growing for the finest and biggest fruit arose in various parts of the country, especially the Midlands and the North; at one time, there were 170 clubs or societies devoted to this. The enthusiasm was such that many people held the opinion that the gooseberry was 'the English fruit' (Roach, 1985). Shows are still held in Cheshire and at Egton Bridge, Yorkshire. The berries are exhibited and assessed, using very old-fashioned units of weight, with a prize going to the heaviest. These clubs were instrumental in developing many of the varieties still grown. Careless was one, raised by a Mr Crompton before 1860. Roach remarks that demand for culinary gooseberries (which are very acid) was stimulated by the abolition of sugar tax in 1874. Shortly after this, a pattern of underplanting top-fruit orchards of plums or apples with gooseberries became important in the Vale of Evesham, Kent and East Anglia. Orchards on this plan, of Bramley apple trees with gooseberries (mostly Careless, but also other British varieties) were established in the Wisbech area of East Anglia. When growers discovered the Careless at a horticultural show in Lancashire in 1897, they brought it home for wholesale adoption. Commercial cultivation of gooseberries has almost died out in the West Midlands, but carries on in East Anglia, where some orchards arranged in the customary manner can still be found.

TECHNIQUE:
Gooseberry bushes are propagated by cuttings; they are cultivated outdoors and the bushes are grown to have a distinct stem so the branches clear the ground. Careless is a variety which requires little specialized pruning, although the bushes are generally encouraged to grow with an open centre, and it is trimmed to control the spreading growth characteristic of this variety. It is moderately vigorous and a heavy cropper, but susceptible to mildew, which is controlled by spraying from April onwards. Protection from birds is required. The fruit is picked by hand in late May and early June.

REGION OF PRODUCTION:
EAST ANGLIA, WISBECH (CAMBRIDGESHIRE); SOUTH EAST ENGLAND.

Conference Pear

A DESSERT AND COOKING PEAR; MEDIUM SIZED, LONG AND TAPERING SHAPE, YELLOWISH GREEN SKIN, EXTENSIVE RUSSETTING (ROUGH AREAS), FIRM TENDER-COARSE FLESH, JUICY, VERY SWEET WHEN RIPE.

HISTORY:

The work of breeding and improvement of pears was really undertaken in continental Europe. With a few exceptions, English varieties have not proved of lasting value.

Two Victorian nurseries which proved exceptions to that rule were Rivers of Sawbridgeworth and Laxton Brothers of Bedford. Thomas Rivers' Conference pear was their most successful creation. It was bred out of a Belgian cooking pear, the Léon le Clare de Laval, and the first orchard was planted at Allington in Kent in 1895 (Roach, 1985). It was exhibited at the International Pear Conference in Chiswick, where it was awarded the only first-class certificate; the judges asked for it to be named in honour of the occasion. A hundred years later, it is still very important in the British market. Conference pears are often cooked, but are also very good dessert pears when ripe.

TECHNIQUE:

The cultivation of pears is similar in principle to that of apples, although the trees can stand less favourable soils but are more temperature-sensitive. They are grafted on quince rootstocks to give dwarf trees and allow for closer planting. Under the old system, trees were planted 4.6m apart each way, with replacement about every 40 years. Developments in orcharding techniques now allow for a distance of 4m one way and 1.8m the other, and replacement every 25 years. Temperature affects the fruit shape of Conference, giving elongated 'naturals' if this is not favourable at flowering time.

REGION OF PRODUCTION:

EAST ANGLIA; SOUTH EAST ENGLAND.

D'Arcy Spice Apple

DESCRIPTION:

A LATE-SEASON DESSERT APPLE, MEDIUM-SIZED, OBLONG, RIBBED, YELLOWISH GREEN TO GOLD WITH BRICK RED FLUSH; OCHRE RUSSETING. FLAVOUR: HOT, SPICY, REMINISCENT OF NUTMEG.

HISTORY:

The first D'Arcy Spice tree was found in the gardens of Tolleshunt d'Arcy Hall (Essex) in the late 1700s. As with many English late-season dessert apples, it has a complex flavour. Though it does not seem to have enjoyed the commercial success of some others, it is locally popular (Morgan & Richards, 1993). It is traditionally picked on Guy Fawkes Day.

REGION OF PRODUCTION:
EAST ANGLIA, ESSEX.

Norfolk Beefing Apple

DESCRIPTION:

A LATE COOKING AND DESSERT APPLE; DIMENSIONS, MEDIUM TO LARGE. FORM IS FLAT-ROUND. THE SKIN, WHICH IS QUITE TOUGH, HAS A DARK PURPLISH FLUSH AND SHORT RED STRIPES OVER GREEN, RIPENING TO CRIMSON OVER GOLD; FLESH IS WHITE, TINGED WITH GREEN. NORFOLK BEEFINGS HAVE A RICH FLAVOUR WHICH, WHEN PRESERVED BY DRYING, IS DESCRIBED AS BEING 'ALMOST OF RAISINS AND CINNAMON'.

HISTORY:

This apple was apparently known in Norfolk by the late eighteenth century, although Beefings are mentioned in correspondence a hundred years earlier. It was a popular variety in the nineteenth century, planted both commercially and in gardens, but had fallen out of favour by 1900. Trees are still to be found in Norfolk (Morgan & Richards, 1993).

Beefings were apples much favoured for drying. They have tough, rather dry flesh and a resilient skin which allows the fruit to be baked without bursting. If they were placed in bread ovens after baking and allowed to dry in the residual heat, they were known as biffins. Throughout the Victorian period, they were dried by Norwich bakers, packed in boxes, and dispatched as presents (mail-order *avant la lettre*) or to London fruiterers (Dickens mentions a window display including biffins in *A Christmas Carol*) – a Christmas delicacy rather in the same style as tangerines were invariable components of the Christmas stockings of our youth.

Their popularity declined, presumably because of changes in technology in the baking industry – gas and electric steel ovens do not have the same good-natured falling heat and availability of the old brick monsters. Even so, they could certainly be found on sale up until the 1950s and may still be produced by private households. Biffins are described by Hartley (1954) as being red, round, and wrinkled, packed down flat in layers. Norwak (1988) recommended that biffins be coated with sugar which had been melted without colouring. 'Black caps' are biffins which have been baked with candied peel, sugar and wine.

Early in the season, the Norfolk Beefing is a cooking apple; after storage until spring, it is sweet enough to eat fresh.

TECHNIQUE:

Cultivation of Norfolk Beefings on a commercial scale has died out, but the trees are still found in gardens. The apples are picked in mid-October and are stored in trays if they are to be eaten fresh. A modern method for making biffins requires whole, unblemished, unpeeled Beefings. They are placed on racks and allowed to dry at a low temperature (about 105°C) for approximately 5 hours. They are removed from the oven and pressed a little to flatten; then returned to the oven for another hour, after which they are removed and allowed to cool. If desired, they can be coated lightly with uncoloured caramel made by melting sugar very gently. The traditional method required them to be left packed in straw layers with a weight on top in the residual heat of a cooling oven.

REGION OF PRODUCTION:
EAST ANGLIA.

Parsnip

DESCRIPTION:

A ROOT WEIGHING BETWEEN 150–300G. COLOUR: PALE CREAM SKIN, WHITE FLESH. FLAVOUR: SWEETISH.

HISTORY:

Parsnips are native to Britain. There are many references to them in Anglo-Saxon documents (they were also marked on the garden plan of the Swiss abbey of St Gall in contemporary Europe) and they continue to be mentioned throughout the Middle Ages, although skirret (*Sium sisarum*), a species of water parsnip and very sweet-tasting, was also a popular culinary root. Parsnips were valued for their own natural sweetness at a time when sugar was expensive. They were used in sweet pies during the sixteenth and seventeenth centuries. They were also more important as a root vegetable before potatoes were widely cultivated. Thomas Cogan wrote at the end of Elizabeth's reign, 'they are common meate among the common people all the time of Autumne, and chiefly upon fish daies'. The cultivation of parsnips and other roots increased enormously to feed the growing population of London during years of bad grain harvests (Thick, 1998).

They never quite shook off their character of food for the poor, and the less intrusive potato was an easier staple and provider of dietary bulk, so that although their use continued: stewed or mashed, roasted, in soups and stocks, in pies, or as a basis for fermented drinks – beer in Northern Ireland, wine in the rest of the country (Cassell's, 1896) –

they have not the cachet of the young turnip or the celeriac, to name 2 other roots (Riley, 1995). They are, however, easy to grow and tolerant of frost. Simon (1960) repeats a bizarre idea that if cooked and cooled and sliced then mixed with mayonnaise, they make a 'Poor Man's Lobster'.

There is a long-standing tradition of cultivating root vegetables in East Anglia, which probably originated with an influx of Dutch religious immigrants who plied their trade as gardeners (those who dug intensively rather than ploughed extensively, a new skill to Tudor Britain) in the sixteenth century. They began to grow roots in the area around Norwich before moving on to the London market and the South-East. Since the eighteenth century, farmers and gardeners in East Anglia and have cultivated turnips, swedes, beets, parsnips and carrots for both local and national consumption, and vegetables are much used in the diet of local people. There is a certain symmetry between the East Anglian supply of human needs and the development of an animal husbandry based on winter-feeding with roots.

TECHNIQUE:

East Anglia includes large areas of free-draining, sandy soils. Easy to work, and allowing the growth of long, straight roots, they are ideal for parsnips and carrots. As a field crop, parsnips are grown from seed planted in November–January. The roots are left in the soil until required; they are now harvested as early as mid-July in response to demand from supermarkets. It is always said that parsnips should not be harvested until they have been exposed to frost. Whilst this is not technically necessary, frost does affect the roots, improving the flavour and making them significantly sweeter. East Anglia has a micro-climate which tends to cold winter weather. As long as the roots are left in the soil until winter, the combination of sandy soil (which reacts quickly to changes in ambient temperature, thus cooling rapidly as the season progresses) and local climate produces well-flavoured parsnips. Several varieties are grown. Some farmers use organic farming techniques; in order to avoid carrot root fly, they drill their parsnips later in the season, and therefore the roots are not ready for harvesting until winter when they have been affected by frost.

REGION OF PRODUCTION:
EAST ANGLIA.

Buckling

DESCRIPTION:
HOT-SMOKED, UNGUTTED HERRING, HEADS REMOVED, ABOUT 18–20CM LONG. WEIGHT: 80–100G. COLOUR: GOLDEN BROWN SKIN, PALE PINK OPAQUE FLESH. FLAVOUR: MILDLY SMOKED.

HISTORY:
Buckling is the name of a cure for herring, *Clupea harengus*. It was first mentioned in English in the early 1900s (*OED*). Grigson (1975) states that it was only after World War II that the cure became familiar in England. Even by 1957, it was possible to write that the cure was not as well known as it should be (Hodgson, 1957). It was German in origin and has been applied to some of the vast quantities of herring processed on the coast of East Anglia, but never seems to have been widely popular (Davidson, 1980).

TECHNIQUE:
The fish are washed and knobbed (gutted and decapitated). Any roe or milt is left in place. Brining is about 45 minutes. They are spitted and assembled on wooden frames, then smoked over hot smoke in small ovens or kilns lined with fire brick. The first part of the cure is to dry the fish in a warm temperature with plenty of draught; then a higher temperature, over a bright fire, is used until they are cooked; finally, they are given the requisite amount of dense smoke, using hardwood sawdust and water, until they are 'an attractive golden colour'.

REGION OF PRODUCTION:
EAST ANGLIA.

A Culinary Celebration of Norfolk

Menu devised by Delia Smith

25th August 2000

When we began to plan this menu for Canary Catering at the Norwich City Football Club, we had no idea if we could actually have everything produced in Norfolk. But we did and all ingredients were sourced locally, including the coffee, which was our trump card. There was actually a special coffee produced in Norfolk, blended with Norfolk wheat!

Canapés of Norfolk Smoked Eel, Bloater Paste and Smoked Salmon with fresh Norfolk Horeseradish

Wild Mushroom Tartlet with Poached Quails' Eggs and Foaming Hollandaise

Potted Crab from Cromer and home-made wholemeal bread (made from locally milled flour)

Confit of Norfolk Duckling with a marmalade of Discovery apples, shallots and Norfolk Cider, runner beans (chosen because the menu was designed for the Olympics!) and gratin of Norfolk Potatoes

Norfolk White Lady and Wissington Ewe's Milk Cheeses with home-made Oat and Raisin Biscuits

Blackcurrant and Oatmeal Torte with blackcurrant ice cream

Coffee with Mini Norfolk Treacle Tarts

Cockle (Stiffkey Blues)

DESCRIPTION:

STIFFKEY BLUES ARE COCKLES, *CARDIUM EDULE*; COLLECTED WHEN THE SHELL IS 25–30MM DIAMETER; THEY ARE SOLD BY WEIGHT OR BY VOLUME, USING THE BRITISH IMPERIAL PINT (APPROXIMATELY 500ML). COLOUR: THE SHELLS VARY FROM PALE LAVENDER TO A DARK GREY-BLUE. FLAVOUR: A RICH SHELLFISH FLAVOUR, REFRESHING AND SLIGHTLY SALTY.

HISTORY:

Cockles were popular beyond Wales; they were much used in British cookery, sent from many coastal towns to industrial cities including London, where they were regarded as a delicacy in the East End. The very cold winter of 1898 killed many cockles and this more general, national, trade seems never to have completely revived. Many of the recipes then current have fallen out of use (Ayrton, 1982). Cockles are gathered at other sites in the British Isles, for example the Thames estuary and the Wash. Processing takes place in several towns, including Leigh on Sea (Essex), Kings Lynn (Norfolk), and Liverpool. An account of the shellfish trade of the Thames estuary makes clear how badly it was affected at the beginning of the last century by a combination of circumstances. Aflalo (1904) wrote, 'Anyone standing beside the heaps of cockle-shells at Leigh and looking forth upon the fishing-boats that lie idle on the mud banks, may easily realise the ruin brought upon once flourishing communities by the inexorable mandates of modern hygiene.'

In 1736, Richard Bradley thought the best cockles he had ever seen were in Torbay, 'as large as a good Oyster'. Two centuries later, Alan Davidson (1989) pronounced, 'the best British cockles are generally held to be the Stiffkey blues'. Stiffkey is a small village on the north Norfolk coast. In fact the written name of this particular cockle is usually spelled as pronounced – stewkey or stookey.

In the 1800s, the women of Stiffkey supplemented their income by gathering from the cockle beds some miles from their homes. This participation of women in the exploitation of the foreshore is a common feature, met in northern France (the flat sands of the Cotentin), the shallows of the River Exe (searching for mussels and oysters), or the deeper, freer-flowing water of the River Dart. The same gender distinction is encountered in the catching and marketing of sea-fish. The men took to the boats, but fishwives carried it inland to sell. As a free food, Stiffkey cockles must have been used for as long as the area has been inhabited, but no records survive. A local government report (1911), commenting on public hygiene, was happy to exclude the cockle beds of Stiffkey from its strictures, so averting the decline experienced in other parts of the estuary. At this time, there were 20–30 women gathering the cockles.

The blue colour has always been thought noteworthy. An alternative, obsolete, name was bluestones. The colour is derived from the anaerobic mud the cockles inhabit.

Domestic cooks steam stewkey blues and use them in soups and pies. They are also boiled and sold from seaside stalls, with pepper and vinegar to taste. Local restaurants serve them with marsh samphire in the season.

TECHNIQUE:

The cockle beds are located several kilometres from Stiffkey, on the seaward side of a salt marsh. The shellfish are gathered from the mud by raking them out; they are then washed and packed in sacks for carriage back to the village. For cleaning, they are immersed in sea water; some people add flour or oatmeal to assist this process. They are opened by steaming. In the Wash, cockles are fished by suction dredging. Locally, worries are expressed about declining numbers and pollution. It is also recognized that the cockle beds unaccountably vanish every few years; possible reasons include the action of the tides washing away the beds or exposing them to seabirds.

REGION OF PRODUCTION:
EAST ANGLIA, NORFOLK.

Crab (Cromer)

DESCRIPTION:

FOR CRABS LANDED ON THE NORFOLK COAST THE MINIMUM CARAPACE WIDTH IS 115MM. IT IS CLAIMED BY INHABITANTS THAT CROMER CRABS ARE NOTICEABLY SWEETER THAN THOSE FISHED ELSEWHERE.

HISTORY:

Oral tradition states that crabs, *Cancer pagurus*, have been fished in the area for centuries; material relating to this was collected by Sally Festing (1977). The reason why the crabs in this area are better than others is not clear, beyond the fact that it lies close to the spawning grounds and the crabs are probably younger than most of those fished in Britain. It is also possible the underwater geography of the area, notably a chalk shelf with runs offshore, influences the feeding of the crabs.

Fishermen on the South coast, parts of the West Country, Wales, the West of Scotland and the North-East all land crabs at local ports and many fishing towns claim them as a speciality. However, special qualities are claimed for those landed in Norfolk. The minimum landing size is smaller than that elsewhere except Cumbria.

TECHNIQUE:

The crabs are caught in pots, brought ashore, measured, and put into fresh water to make them drowsy, before scrubbing and boiling. They may be sold whole, or dressed by picking the body and claws, cleaning the shell, and packing the meat back into it.

REGION OF PRODUCTION:
EAST ANGLIA, CROMER (NORFOLK)

Mussel (England)

DESCRIPTION:

MINIMUM LENGTH IS 50MM; THE CULTIVATED MUSSELS ARE RELIABLY FATTENED AND WELL-FLAVOURED.

HISTORY:

Fisheries for mussels are found on the East, South and West coasts of Britain. In East Anglia, Harwich was an important eighteenth-century centre of the trade (Cutting, 1955). Although some sophisticated recipes appear in early cookery books, mussels were generally considered food of the poor. At Brancaster (Norfolk), oral tradition states the fishery has been there for as long as anyone can remember, and in the late nineteenth century, local fishermen leased beds for mussel and oyster cultivation from the lord of the manor. A committee to regulate the Norfolk mussel fishery was formed in the late nineteenth century, as local farmers had started to exploit the beds as a source of fertilizer, threatening stocks. Recently, there has been a shortage of mussels in the Wash, possibly due to a drop in fertility as a consequence of a reduction in the minimum size allowed to be fished.

TECHNIQUE:

In East Anglia, the 'mussel seed' (mussels about 1 year old) are collected by hand from sandbanks in the Wash and taken to Brancaster. Here, the fishermen put them in the lays – short stretches of foreshore along tidal creeks – to fatten in the nutrient-rich water. The lays are small and are carefully maintained by cleaning the mussel beds of mud, which accumulates as the shellfish grow, before new stocks are laid. They are harvested by hand at 2–3 years and purified under ultra-violet light, graded, and sold fresh.

REGION OF PRODUCTION:

EAST ANGLIA, BRANCASTER (NORFOLK)

Potted Crab

DESCRIPTION:

CRAB PASTE, PRESERVED IN BUTTER, SOLD BY WEIGHT IN SMALL POTS OR TUBS OF 100–200G. COLOUR: A LIGHT REDDISH BROWN. FLAVOUR: CRAB, WITH SPICES AND BUTTER.

HISTORY:

This falls into the long tradition of preserving meat and fish under a layer of melted butter in a shallow container. Small game birds and some types of fish were preserved whole or in large pieces, but usually the flesh was cooked, picked from the bones and pounded to a paste. This was common practice in eighteenth-century households. Peggy Gates, housekeeper to the Northumberland gentleman Henry Ellison in the 1720s, 'had a reputation for potted charrs, goose-pie, potted woodcock and grouse, and bottled mushrooms' (Hughes, 1952).

These preserves were commercialized from an early date, but during the nineteenth century, the process entered a semi-industrial phase as fish or meat pastes, sealed in small jars, became part of a grocer's stock in trade and reached an ever broader public as sandwiches became a staple at midday and at teatime. The entry given to them in *Law's Grocer's Manual* (*c*. 1895) suggests they were not highly regarded and they have continued to suffer from a poor image. However, they remained popular, and were widely available.

The development of commodities such as potted crab or potted shrimps has avoided some of the odium cast upon meat and fish pastes. The latter were wholly industrial, often using the detritus of more wholesome commerce, offering pungent flavour at minimal cost. Potting crab or shrimps, like potting char, was a means of preserving a coastal delicacy for sale inland. There is a long tradition of potting crab on the East coast of Britain, as indeed can be found in other regions.

The popularity of such stratagems in our day has been stimulated by the advance of domestic food processors, delivering a texture suitable for potting without the grim labour. It has enabled small companies to enter the field, while other technologies have eased distribution and storage.

TECHNIQUE:

The crabs are cooked, cooled, and all edible meat is removed and carefully separated from shell and cartilage. The meat is mixed with butter and spices – black pepper, mace and cayenne are customary –

then blended in a processor. Similar products are made, based on other fish, especially herring roes, smoked mackerel, and fresh or smoked salmon or trout. Smoked salmon is usually potted without being cooked first, often blended with cream cheese. The deep layer of butter that used to be essential no longer is.

REGION OF PRODUCTION:
East Anglia.

Red Herring

DESCRIPTION:
RED HERRING ARE LEFT UNSPLIT, WITH THEIR HEADS ON, AND WEIGH ABOUT 300–350G. THE COLOUR IS A BRIGHT PINK-RED. THEY HAVE A HARD, DRY TEXTURE, VERY CONCENTRATED FLAVOUR.

HISTORY:
Herring curing has a long history in East Anglia. The fish were landed in the ports along the coast in vast quantities – in 1902–3 over 500 million herring were caught by Yarmouth boats – and subjected to curing processes intended to preserve them for many months under conditions of uncertain hygiene. Of these cures, that used for red herring is one of the older and more rigorous.

Great Yarmouth (Norfolk) has always been an important fishery. There were 24 fishermen recorded living there in the Domesday Book. Excavations have revealed a tremendous range of fish bones – of all the species caught there today – from the Anglo-Saxon period, mute witness of many fishy feasts. Investigations elsewhere in East Anglia have revealed an apparent increase in the presence of herring at about the time of the Norman conquest – the fish has always been subject to notorious shifts and migrations (Hagen, 1995). Doubtless, the town's pre-eminence in the trade dates from the same period. The household of Katherine de Norwich, a Norfolk widow in the 1330s, was buying great numbers of herrings – red, white (bloaters) and fresh – from Yarmouth (Woolgar, 1992) and this pattern was repeated across the country. The connection was celebrated by a town fair, already going in the Middle Ages, which ran through the month of October (Mabey, 1978).

The poet Thomas Nashe, a native of Lowestoft, wrote 'Lenten Stuffe, or the Praise of the Red Herring' recounting the legend that a Yarmouth man discovered red herring accidentally when he hung his excess catch from the rafters where, in the smoke of the fire, they turned from white to red. While the first customers for red herrings may have been English folk needing to eat fish on fast days, trade never fell away with a change in religion or politics because new buyers were continually appearing. First there were the Catholics of mainland Europe; then the fish was found a convenient food for the slave traders to offer their captives in transit (thus entering into the African and Afro-Caribbean culinary repertoire); then it carved out a market for its particular flavour in Asia.

Modern refrigeration means that the heavy cures used for red herring are unnecessary for the British, and only a few are produced for those who still have a taste for such strong, salty food. However, exports continue, although even these cures tend to be lighter than formerly. Variant names reflect the nature of the cure: 'high dries' on the one hand, 'golden herring' for something lighter. They were also called 'militiamen' (referring to the red coats) in Yarmouth. Their Scottish sobriquet was 'Glasgow Magistrates' – reference perhaps to a match of facial hue and herring skin.

TECHNIQUE:

Autumn fish with a fat content of about 15 per cent are required: this is important – not enough and they dry out, too much and they go rancid. These are fish landed in October–November. The fish are left whole. The closest cure to the traditional red herring made today is: dry salt for about 2 days, then over cold smoke for 4–6 weeks, after which the fish are removed from the kiln and packed. For lighter cures, brined fish are smoked for 3–7 days, depending on the market for which they are destined.

Smoked Sprats

DESCRIPTION:

WHOLE, UNGUTTED HOT-SMOKED FISH. A KILO OF SMOKED SPRATS
CONTAINS APPROXIMATELY 40 FISH. COLOUR: GOLDEN. FLAVOUR: RICH,
OILY, SMOKED.

HISTORY:

Sprats, *Sprattus sprattus*, are caught in waters beyond the Thames
estuary. The fish were once caught in stow-nets, wide-necked traps held
stationary against the tide. It was a technique at least as old as the Tudor
period. The catches were at times enormous. In the 1870s there were
600 boats working the Thames estuary; they were landing anything up
to 130 tons a day at Billingsgate in the 1860s (Dyson, 1977).

For centuries the fishing towns of the Suffolk coast have been
preserving their catch. An early reference in Defoe (1724–6) speaks of
sprats being cured in Southwold and Dunwich by being made red, as
herrings were at Yarmouth. The author of *The Art and Mystery of
Curing, Preserving and Potting* (1864) gives 2 methods for curing
sprats, including a method for 'redding' which he called Aldeburgh
smoked sprats (Aldeburgh being one of the towns at which the fish
were landed). Later, *Law's Grocer's Manual* remarked that sprats 'are
found in immense shoals on many parts of our coasts during the latter
part of the year ... often remarkably abundant, especially off the coast
of Suffolk, Essex and Kent. They are often cleaned and cured by being
soaked in brine and finally dried, or smoked, for sale in small bundles
of 30, or put in small wood boxes.' The men at Brightlingsea (Essex)
both smoked the sprats for the home market and packed them in
barrels with salt and spices for export to Holland (Dyson, 1977).

Sprats have long been a particular delicacy in England, much as
sardines in more southerly countries, or whitebait – a taste that was at

its height in the Victorian period. Sala (1859) wrote, 'I don't think there is … a more charming red-letter night in the calendar of gastronomy, than a sprat supper. You must have three pennyworth of sprats, a large tablecloth is indispensable for finger-wiping purposes – for he who would eat sprats with a knife and fork is unworthy the name of epicure – and after the banquet I should recommend … the absorption of a petit verre of the best Hollands.'

TECHNIQUE:

Sprats are landed in the small fishing ports of the Suffolk coast in late autumn, the season beginning in November. The fish are picked over and given a short brining before they are threaded by hand on hooks and suspended in cold smoke for a short time. As with other smoked fish, the exact length of time depends on the oil content of the fish and ambient temperature. The temperature of the smoke is then increased and the fish smoked briefly in hot smoke to cook through. After cooling, the smoked sprats keep for about a week.

Some fresh sprats are frozen, to be thawed and smoked later in the year, when fresh fish of the correct oil content are not available.

A now outmoded method called for 4 hours of brining, a period of draining and the fishes to be smoked until they were 'the colour of Spanish mahogany', after which they were packed for export.

REGION OF PRODUCTION:

EAST ANGLIA, SOUTHWOLD AND ALDEBURGH (SUFFOLK).

Yarmouth Bloater

DESCRIPTION:

COLD-SMOKED UNGUTTED HERRING, ABOUT 30CM LONG. WEIGHT: 350–400G. COLOUR: SILVERY GOLD SKIN, DARK PINK TRANSLUCENT FLESH. FLAVOUR: MILDLY SMOKED, FISHY, SLIGHTLY GAMEY.

HISTORY:

Bloater indicates a specific type of cure used for herring, *Clupea harengus*. Yarmouth bloaters were first noted in the early nineteenth century, but 'bloat herring' are mentioned 2 centuries earlier. The description bloat or bloater is conjectured to have links with Scandinavian languages, indicating either fish that had a soft texture, or fish which had undergone a steeping process (*OED*).

Yarmouth legend has it that the process was discovered by accident when a fish curer threw salt over fresh herrings to preserve them temporarily. But the date given for this supposed event is later than the date of the first quotation in the *Oxford English Dictionary*. Although the evolution of the process is a matter for conjecture, the fame of the product is not. *Law's Grocer's Manual* (*c.* 1895) was firm in its praise. Bloater paste, a favourite Victorian spread for toast, was made by skinning, cleaning and mincing the fish, mixing with lard and spices, and pressing into fancy pots, patent jars or tins, which were hermetically sealed. Because the mild cure results in fish that will not keep for very long, paste was a convenient means of extending the range of the trade. None the less, manufacture remains the preserve of the immediate area round Yarmouth. Refrigeration allows wider distribution.

TECHNIQUE:
Bloaters are only made at a time of the year when the herring have the correct oil content, commonly the autumn. Fish landed at East Anglian ports are preferred. The time spent in the salt brine varies, but about 2 hours is typical. The fish are suspended on spits of wood pushed through the gills and hung in cool smoke from hardwood sawdust for 12–18 hours.

REGION OF PRODUCTION:
EAST ANGLIA, GREAT YARMOUTH (NORFOLK).

Newmarket Sausages

DESCRIPTION:
FRESH PORK SAUSAGE (65–70 PER CENT PORK); EACH 10CM LONG, AND 8 SAUSAGES TO THE LB (450G). COLOUR: DEEP PINK-BEIGE WITH A FEW FLECKS OF HERB. FLAVOUR: MODERATELY SPICY, WITH A FAIRLY DRY TEXTURE.

Newmarket, east of Cambridge, is best known for horse racing. It appears its sausage developed as a souvenir. No doubt fresh sausages have been made in the area for centuries, but the Newmarket sausage as known today appears to have a shorter history. It was first made in the 1880s. There are 3 butchers in the town who sell 'Newmarket' sausages, each one producing a slightly different version. This much is certain.

There are various claims to the original coarse-cut, pork-based sausage with a secret spicing mix. One maker, Grant Powter, uses a recipe invented by his great-grandfather, William Harper, who was apprenticed to a butcher in Newmarket in the 1880s. The company of Musk's say that their recipe was evolved by James Musk in 1884. Whatever the truth, the sausages are now firmly established.

TECHNIQUE:

Powter's selects heavier-grade pigs from local sources; the carcass is hand-boned and meat from all parts used in the sausages. It is minced coarsely, mixed with rusk and a fairly spicy, piquant seasoning made to a secret family formula, plus salt, and then filled into natural casings and hand-linked.

Musk's use a 'heavy' old-fashioned bread, made for them by a baker in a neighbouring village, in place of the rusk; they too use meat from the whole pig in their sausages. Neither uses preservatives or artificial colourings.

REGION OF PRODUCTION:

EAST ANGLIA, NEWMARKET (SUFFOLK).

Norfolk Black Turkey

DESCRIPTION:

NORFOLK BLACKS HAVE BLACK FEATHERS AND MATURE SLOWLY TO GIVE HENS WEIGHING ABOUT 4.5–6.8KG AND STAGS OF 7.2–10.5KG. THE SKIN HAS A DISTINCTIVE BLACK PITTING OF DARK FEATHER STUMPS.

FLAVOUR IS MEATIER AND MORE INTENSE THAN THAT OF
COMMERCIAL HYBRIDS.

East Anglia has always been important for its cereal crops. After the
harvest was gathered, poultry were fattened on the stubble. 'In the
seventeenth century, great flocks of turkeys (often five hundred or
more) were driven more than a hundred miles down the rough roads
to the London markets. Their feet were bound in rags and dipped in
tar to prevent damage, and each night they would be penned in fields
by the roadside where they could feast on the remains of the corn in
the autumn stubble' (Norwak, 1988).

Turkeys are not indigenous but were brought back from Mexico
in the sixteenth century. The fact their name suggests they came
from the East not the West is all of a piece with the confusion of
new consumers, who were faced at the same time with the guinea
fowl – also called turkey in the first instance. Another introduction,
maize, was called Turkey corn in a similar muddle about origin. The
historian Sir Richard Baker (1643) claimed the bird came into the
country in 1524, citing a rhyme that went, 'Turkeys, carps, hoppes,
piccarell, and beer, Came into England all in one year.' The fact that
this is quite wrong about the fishes need not make it completely
mistaken about the turkey. In the 50 years from their probable
introduction, they had penetrated as far as the East Anglian table of
Thomas Tusser (1573) who wrote of the Christmas board laden
with 'pig, veale, goose and capon, and turkey well drest'. The
progressive ousting of the goose had begun and the replacement of
the bustard, the peacock and other 'great birds' of medieval feasts
was assured.

As Kent was the garden and orchard, so Suffolk and Norfolk were
the grain and meat larder of London. The Norfolk Black was the
historic race of turkeys fattened by East Anglian farmers, but there
have always been two principal strains of turkey in this country. The
Norfolk is the smaller, perhaps the less hardy. The other is the

Cambridge, which has a more varied plumage. The Cambridge has been crossed many times with the American Bronze, the largest of the turkey kind, giving rise to the present breed of Cambridge Bronze. In recent years, Cambridge and Norfolks have been crossed themselves. The result is the Kelly Bronze, which combines slow maturation, good flavour and more breast meat than is usual in Norfolk Blacks. It is sometimes held the two English strains represent a double introduction. The Cambridge represents the turkey of Mexico, brought over by the Spaniards; the Norfolk that of north-east America, now the United States and Canada, which may have been carried in English or French boats.

The pure-bred Norfolk Black's rarity in modern Britain has been caused by constant hybridization: growers sought greater productivity and a different conformation once turkey entered the mass-market food supply. The Norfolk Black grows slowly, and supermarkets insist on a bird with a white skin. Consumers also favour a plump breast. However, one large flock of Norfolk Blacks was maintained by the Peel family, farmers in East Anglia, when the breed was virtually forgotten for commercial purposes. It is now raised on a small scale by farmers and smallholders in the area.

TECHNIQUE:

There is no particular method attached to rearing Norfolk Blacks, but the small scale on which they are farmed means that many are free-range, feeding in the fields, their diet supplemented with grain. They are killed at 25 weeks and dry-plucked. The Traditional Farm Fresh Turkey Association recommends hanging for a minimum of 7 days; in practice, many producers give up to 14 days.

REGION OF PRODUCTION:

EAST ANGLIA.

In Norfolk, dumplings were originally called 'floaters' because they were traditionally made with bread dough (containing yeast) rather than suet, and thus they float rather than sink. Many people now mix suet with flour when making dumplings, although the suet variety used to be derided by Norfolk men as 'sinkers' and dumplings when properly cooked the Norfolk way should be as light as a feather.

It is traditional to have dumplings with stews or with boiled beef or boiled bacon. When meat used to be an expensive luxury, many families ate dumplings (much as others ate Yorkshire puddings) before the main meat course, the idea being that the dumplings would blunt the appetite and so less meat would be needed.

When making Norfolk dumplings, the traditional methods should be followed. Wives of Norfolk farmers used to make them to weigh exactly four ounces each. Today, they are still made from proved bread dough (dough left to rise in a warm place) rolled into balls and then left to prove again before being slipped into a large saucepan of fast-boiling water and boiled with the lid on for twenty minutes. The lid should never be lifted during the cooking time and the dumplings should then be served immediately with gravy. Traditionally, dumplings should not be cut with a knife, but torn apart with two forks at once so that they do not become too heavy. As I said earlier, many people now use suet when making dumplings and instead of cooking them separately in boiling water steam them over a pan of boiling water or over the top of a casserole, or even throw them into the casserole for the last twenty minutes of cooking, but this results in a much heavier dumpling.

Galton Blackiston

CHEF AND PROPRIETOR, MORSTON HALL, MORSTON

Norfolk Dumplings

450G (1 LB) PLAIN FLOUR

1 TSP SALT

4 TBSP CHOPPED PARSLEY

15G (½ OZ) FRESH YEAST

1 TSP CASTER SUGAR

150ML (¼ PINT) WARM WATER

2 TBSP WARM MILK

Place the flour, salt and chopped parsley into the bowl of a food mixer and, using the mixer's dough hook, mix thoroughly. Combine the yeast and sugar in a bowl and mix with your fingertips so that the yeast breaks down and becomes smooth and almost liquid. Add the water and milk to the yeast, and mix this together well.

With the food mixer still running, slowly add the yeast mixture to the flour. Allow the machine to knead the dough for five to eight minutes, or until it comes away from the sides of the bowl.

Remove the bowl from the mixer and cover the dough with a clean, damp tea towel, then leave it in a warm place for about one hour or until the dough has doubled in volume.

Turn the dough out onto a lightly floured surface, knead well with the palm of your hand and then form into eight dumplings. Place the dumplings on a tray and leave them to prove again in a warm place.

Bring a large saucepan of water to a rolling boil and, once the dumplings have proved again, slip them quickly into the boiling water. Place the lid on the saucepan and boil for exactly twenty minutes.

Using a slotted spoon, remove the dumplings from the boiling water. Serve immediately either on their own with some gravy or to accompany boiled beef, boiled bacon or a casserole.

Suffolk Ham

DESCRIPTION:

A CURED SMOKED HAM. WHOLE HAMS WEIGH 6.3–8KG. THE BEER CURE YIELDS A DEEP BLACKISH-BROWN SKIN, THE CIDER CURE A PALER, MOTTLED COLOUR. THEY HAVE A STRONG, SWEET HAM FLAVOUR, LIGHTER WHEN THE CIDER CURE IS USED.

HISTORY:

In 1838 Suffolk hams were spoken of with approval by a contributor to the *Magazine of Domestic Economy*, who considered this county made the best in England. The cure was similar to that used today. First the hams were rubbed with plain salt and left for a short time; then a pickle was composed of salt, saltpetre, coarse brown sugar, strong old beer and spices. These were boiled together until thick and syrupy and rubbed into the hams which then lay for 5 weeks, after which they were dried and smoked. Although Mrs Beeton (1861) gave a 'Suffolk Recipe' for pickling hams, hers was a dry-salt cure, including sugar and vinegar, unlike others quoted. In the early twentieth century a wet pickle using stout was being used by various manufacturers, including the Jerrey family, now into the third generation using the recipe – with the original smokehouse as well. In the past, several farms and companies in the Suffolk area made hams by this cure but their number has diminished since the Second World War.

TECHNIQUE:

The pork legs are selected for a specified level of fat. They are brined in salt, saltpetre and water, then pickled in a mixture of black treacle, sugar, salt and stout or cider for 3–4 weeks. Smoking takes place for 5 days over oak sawdust. They are matured for at least one month. Farmhouse methods involved 3 days' dry-salting before the hams were immersed in the sweet pickle; the hams were considered to be at their best when between 1 and 2 years old.

REGION OF PRODUCTION:

EAST ANGLIA, SUFFOLK.

Suffolk Sweet-Cured Bacon

DESCRIPTION:

SMOKED CURED PORK FOR COOKING. COLOUR: THE PICKLE MAKES THE OUTSIDE VERY DARK; THE FAT HAS A VERY SLIGHT BROWN CAST AND THE LEAN IS A DEEP PINK-RED. FLAVOUR: DISTINCTLY SWEET, WITH HINT OF MOLASSES, BUT ALSO VERY SALTY, UNDERPINNED WITH A SLIGHT ACID NOTE.

HISTORY:

The word 'bacon' meant back. It was only transferred to its exclusive application to the cured backs of pigs in mute recognition of a constant of British food culture. A similar transference may be seen in the word 'brawn', which once applied to the flesh of any animal (or human), but in culinary terms was progressively restricted to that of the wild boar and then of the pig.

It is the use of a sweet cure, similar to that used for hams, which distinguishes this from other artisanal bacon. How long it has been used is unknown. Suffolk bacon was discussed in 1838 by a contributor to the *Magazine of Domestic Economy*, who obviously thought highly of it, but considered Buckinghamshire made finer. The use of a similar pickle is a tradition in the family of Nigel Jerrey, one of the present makers, dating back at least 75 years. The bacon should be grilled rather than fried.

TECHNIQUE:

The cure of the 1840s was similar to today's: salt and coarse brown sugar applied hot to the flitches. This is just as for Suffolk ham, but bacon is cut from the back and belly. As the joints are thinner, the meat is not pickled as long as the hams. It is smoked after curing.

REGION OF PRODUCTION:

EAST ANGLIA, SUFFOLK.

Pressed Tongue (Suffolk Cure)

DESCRIPTION:

CURED AND COOKED OX TONGUES CURLED TO FIT A CYLINDRICAL
MOULD 18–20CM DIAMETER. CUT IN THIN SLICES. COLOUR: DEEP PINK
WITH SMALL WHITE FLECKS, SURROUNDED BY AMBER JELLY; DARK
EXTERIOR. FLAVOUR: HIGHLY SALTED, WITH A RICH TEXTURE.

HISTORY:

Tongue has long been a valued part of the offal from cattle, although
the fact that it is generally referred to as coming from the ox (the
Anglo-Saxon word for cattle) as opposed to beef (from the Norman
French *boeuf*, which was adopted into English to mean ox-flesh once
it became meat on the overlord's table) indicates that it may not have
been considered amongst the choicest parts of the animal. Early
recipes show tongues cured in much the same way as salt beef or
bacon, using dry salt and saltpetre and spices or herbs. After the meat
had been pickled 7–10 days, it was dried and smoked (David, 1970).

Acton (1845) gave 'A Suffolk Receipt' for curing tongue which
included coarse sugar and was similar to that still used for curing
bacon. This early confirmation of a regional particularity was endorsed
by Webb (c. 1930) in her study of the curing of meat, including
tongue, in East Anglia.

Processed tongues were sold in various forms: straight from the
cure, dried and smoked, or cooked and pressed by the butcher. The
latter is now by far the most common. Suffolk-cured tongues can be
obtained today from specialist suppliers. 'Lunch tongues' are a name
for pigs' or sheep's tongues, brined, cooked and moulded in similar
fashion. The name perhaps reveals the favoured time for eating these
meats, often with salad or in sandwiches. When hot, a Cumberland or
cherry sauce is a recognized accompaniment.

TECHNIQUE:

Initial preparation requires tongues to be washed thoroughly and
trimmed at the root. They are brined in a salt, saltpetre and brown
sugar pickle for 3 weeks, then simmered in fresh water for about 4

hours. As soon as they are cool enough to handle, any remaining bone and gristle is trimmed from the root and the skin carefully removed. The tongue is curled to fit a circular mould with a little aspic jelly. A cover is placed on top and the meat pressed until absolutely cold, then it is unmoulded and cut in very thin slices. A butcher may prepare several tongues at once in a mould deep enough to accommodate them.

Brines or pickles for tongue are basically the same as those for bacon and ham, with small regional variations in salt and sugar content. It seems that producers do not smoke tongues now; this was a preservation method of the past which canning and freezing have made unnecessary. Consumers have lost the taste for heavily salted and smoked meat.

REGION OF PRODUCTION:
EAST ANGLIA, SUFFOLK

Norfolk Knob

DESCRIPTION:
ROUND RUSKS WITH A HOLLOW CENTRE, 40MM DIAMETER, 30MM DEEP. WEIGHT: 12G. COLOUR: PALE GOLD TOP AND BOTTOM, WITH A DISTINCT PALE BAND AROUND THE MIDDLE. FLAVOUR AND TEXTURE: SLIGHTLY SWEET, LIGHT, VERY CRISP AND FRIABLE.

HISTORY:
These little rolls, also known as hollow cakes, are biscuits in the true sense of being twice baked (Latin *bis coctum*, French *bis cuit*). Norwak (1988) mentions the connections East Anglia has had with the Netherlands, suggesting they influenced the development of rusk-like breads in this area; similar biscuits, but smaller and richer, are made in Suffolk. James Woodforde, a Norfolk parson, records a gift of hollow cakes in 1788. Grigson (1984) quotes a recipe from 1821. According to Mr Ashworth, the baker best known for the product, the name 'Norfolk Knob' was the invention of a bakery company called

Stannard, who traded in Norwich for about a century until the 1970s. The local name is 'hollow biscuits'; this use of the word biscuit in its original sense suggests a long history. It is always said that King George VI, when staying on his estate at Sandringham, would order a supply. To eat, the knobs are first broken in half by twisting, then spread with butter, jam or cheese.

TECHNIQUE:

A yeast-leavened dough of flour and water with a little fat and sugar is used. Cold water is preferred, as it stops the mixture rising too quickly. The dough is rolled, folded once, docked, then rolled by hand into 20mm circles. Once proved, they are baked for 15 minutes at 190°C. The knobs are cooled then dried out in a low oven for about 2 hours. Some domestic recipes are chemically leavened.

REGION OF PRODUCTION:

EAST ANGLIA, WYMONDHAM (NORFOLK).

Custard Tart

DESCRIPTION:

AN OPEN ROUND TART WITH SLOPING SIDES AND CRIMPED EDGES; 70MM ACROSS THE TOP, 45MM ACROSS BASE, 20–30MM DEEP; LARGER SIZES ARE MADE, USUALLY STRAIGHT-SIDED AND SHALLOWER. WEIGHT: 100G. COLOUR: YELLOW SPECKLED WITH BROWN. FLAVOUR AND TEXTURE: RICH, EGGY AND SWEET, SMOOTH TEXTURED, SPICED WITH NUTMEG.

HISTORY:

From medieval times, pastry cases containing spiced custard (a mixture of eggs and milk or cream) have been baked in Britain. A *crustarde lumbarde*, or open pie containing spices, sugar and dried fruit, appeared in one of the earliest cookery manuscripts dating from *c.* 1390. Such sweet custards have been flavoured with bay leaves, cinnamon or lemon, made into puddings to be boiled in a cloth, or baked in moulds or cooked in pastry. A group of rich custard recipes appears to belong to the Cambridge and Norfolk area. An example is 'the Charter', a baked custard of cream and eggs served with apricots, traced by Jane Grigson (1984) to a Norwich recipe of the 1820s. Burnt cream, another rich custard served under a layer of caramelized sugar, is claimed by various Cambridge colleges. White (1932) gives a recipe for tartlets of pastry made with ground almonds filled with cream custard, remarking that these were favourites with Cambridge undergraduates in the 1890s; they were called cream darioles. Dariole originally meant a small pastry case with various fine fillings. It has come to refer to the small tin moulds, rather deep with steeply flared sides, similar in shape to the foil dishes used by commercial bakers to hold custard tarts even now.

TECHNIQUE:

An unsweetened short-crust pastry is generally used with flour and fat (lard) in the proportions 2:1. A mould is lined, a custard (the richer ones use cream rather than milk) is poured to the top, and nutmeg is sprinkled over the surface. Richer custards contain more egg yolks; plainer ones may include cornflour.

REGION OF PRODUCTION:
EAST ANGLIA.

Cider (Eastern Tradition)

DESCRIPTION:

CIDER FROM EASTERN ENGLAND TENDS TO BE LESS PERFUMED THAN THAT FROM THE WEST, WITH A NUTTY DRYNESS AND MARKED ACIDITY. IT IS 7.5–8 PER CENT ALCOHOL BY VOLUME (6 PER CENT IN THE WEST).

HISTORY:

Some of the earliest records of cider in Britain come from the East. Wilson (1973) mentions Sussex and Kent as cider-making areas in the twelfth century, and Norfolk in the early thirteenth century. Its history was affected by factors similar to those which influenced the drink in the West Country, with one important difference. The interest in apples specifically for making cider which developed in Herefordshire during the 1600s never really penetrated east. Consequently, the tradition is to use whatever apples are available. The industry is smaller than in the South West.

TECHNIQUE:
The method used is the same as that in the West; the significant difference being the apple varieties. Bramleys provide the bulk.

REGION OF PRODUCTION:
SOUTH AND EAST ENGLAND.

'I hate a man who swallows it, affecting not to know what he is eating. I suspect his taste in higher matters.'
CHARLES LAMB, *ESSAYS OF ELIA*

Old Ale (East Anglia): Strong Suffolk

DESCRIPTION:
DARK, RICH RED-BROWN IN COLOUR; A TOASTY, WINY, BITTER FLAVOUR. IT IS 6 PER CENT ALCOHOL BY VOLUME.

HISTORY:
The brewery producing Strong Suffolk is in Bury St Edmunds. Barley has long been a major crop here, and malting is a local industry. The Greene King brewery dates from the late 1700s, although the town has a history of brewing stretching back over a thousand years. Strong Suffolk has been produced since the early twentieth century. It is regarded as a type of old ale, but it differs from most beers in this style because it is produced by an early, but now very unusual technique of blending 2 beers together, one of which is aged in wooden vats.

TECHNIQUE:
Strong Suffolk is a blend of 2 beers, neither of which is sold on its

own. The brewery uses water from its own wells, and makes most of its own malt from East Anglian barley; English hops are used exclusively. One of the beers used in the blend is known as 5X: this is brewed to an original gravity of 105, fermented, then transferred to oak vats which are sealed and covered with a layer of Suffolk marl (a local clay containing carbonate of lime, once used as a soil improver and fertilizer). This acts as a filter, against contamination by wild yeasts and other harmful microflora. The beer matures in these vats for 1–3 years, developing a spicy flavour and gradually increasing in alcoholic content. 5X is blended with a full-bodied malty beer called BPA, which is brewed as required and used after a short period of warm conditioning.

REGION OF PRODUCTION:
EAST ANGLIA.

Cider Vinegar

DESCRIPTION:
CIDER VINEGAR IS CLEAR AND ORANGE-YELLOW. THE FLAVOUR IS ACID WITH DISTINCT CIDER OVERTONES. IT IS NORMALLY ABOUT 5-5.5 PER CENT ACID.

HISTORY:
Formerly, almost every town would support at least one vinegar brewer and regional differences were more marked, reflecting local methods of making beer or cider. Cider-makers found vinegar all too easy to make accidentally, since apple juice left to ferment alone can easily develop into vinegar. In the mid-nineteenth century one comment was that much vinegar was 'made in Devonshire and America from refuse cider'. Although many cidermen still make a little vinegar in this casual way, since the 1950s, large-scale production is controlled by using an acetator.

The 2 largest cider-makers producing vinegar are in East Anglia and the South-East. One is Aspall's, founded in 1728 when a member of the Chevallier-Guilders family moved to Suffolk from Jersey, bringing cider-apple trees with him.

TECHNIQUE:
Cider is fermented by the English method. After resting, it undergoes acetous fermentation in which cultured bacteria are introduced under controlled conditions. Aspall's, which produces an organic vinegar, uses a Green Shield acetator; Merrydown uses a Fring. The vinegar is matured for several weeks before filtering, dilution to specified acid content and bottling.

REGION OF PRODUCTION:
EAST AND SOUTH ENGLAND.

Colman's Mustard

DESCRIPTION:
MUSTARD POWDER IS LIGHT YELLOW IN COLOUR AND, FRESHLY MIXED, HOT AND PUNGENT TO TASTE, MELLOWING ON STORAGE. THE INGREDIENTS ARE MUSTARD FLOUR, WHEAT FLOUR, SALT AND TURMERIC.

HISTORY:
The manufacture of mustard powder has, for about a century, been almost synonymous with the firm of Colman's in Norwich, which has developed a product based on particular strains of mustard seed. Colman's has forged close relationships with specified growers to ensure continuity of quality and supply.

The original creation of dry mustard powder by Mrs Clements of Durham did not long remain her sole monopoly. Producers sprang up all over the country during the 1700s, one of the most important being the London firm of Keen & Company – hence the phrase 'keen as mustard'. Manufacture in Durham eventually ceased.

The fact that mustard began one segment of its history in Durham was no coincidence: that county grew a lot of the plant and therefore had an industry to process or grind its seeds. Likewise, the rise of

Colman's of Norwich was a reflection of agricultural reality. Jeremiah Colman acquired a flour mill which also ground mustard seed. The business grew, enhanced by clever advertising and careful quality control. By the end of the century, *Law's Grocer's Manual* observed that no other country in the world carried on the preparation of mustard as energetically as England. Colman's bought Keen's and several other mustard companies in the early twentieth century and now dominates the market.

TECHNIQUE:

Mustard has been grown in East Anglia for a long time but, after World War II, Colman's developed strains of brown and white mustard for their own use, and improved agricultural methods associated with the crop. Much of the skill in producing mustard lies in blending the correct proportions of various types of seed.

Colman's formula is closely guarded. Brown and white seeds come from specified growers, their entire crop acquired by Colman's. It is cleaned, dried, crushed with steel rollers and sifted to remove the husks. The flours are blended, wheat flour and turmeric added, the mixture packed in tins. The pungency is enhanced by the product not being heat-treated.

REGION OF PRODUCTION:

EAST ANGLIA.

Maldon Sea Salt

DESCRIPTION:

MALDON SALT IS WHITE, WITH A SOFT, FLAKY TEXTURE. ITS FLAVOUR IS CLEAN, SHARP AND FREE FROM BITTERNESS. THE MALDON PROCESS RESULTS IN A PYRAMID-SHAPED CRYSTAL. ONLY THE MALDON CRYSTAL SALT COMPANY PRODUCES THIS PARTICULAR TYPE.

HISTORY:

Sea salt has been extracted at various sites around the British coasts for thousands of years. The southern coast of East Anglia is flat, with salt marshes and tidal inlets well-suited to salt extraction. In the Domesday Book (1086), 45 salt pans are listed in the Maldon area. In the Middle Ages, salt was extracted by boiling sea-water in 'leddes' (lead pans). References to these are found in wills of the sixteenth century. In the eighteenth century, Mrs Glasse (1747) mentioned salt from 'Malding' in Essex as a large, clear salt which gave meat a fine flavour.

The present company grew from a salt works established in 1823; it became the Maldon Crystal Salt Company in the 1880s.

TECHNIQUE:

Sea water is collected from salt marshes when the salt content is at its maximum, after a period of dry weather at the spring tides. It is kept in holding tanks and allowed to settle before being filtered and pumped into storage tanks. It is then drawn off into pans about 3 metres square, mounted on a system of brick flues. The water is brought to a rapid boil and skimmed. The heat is reduced to just below boiling point and the water allowed to evaporate, concentrating the salt in minute, pyramid-like structures. When the quantity of crystals in the remaining water reaches the surface of the liquid, heating is stopped. The pans are cooled and the salt harvested by raking it to one side with wooden hoes. It is then drained in special bins for 48 hours and drying is completed in a salt store. Before packing, the humidity of the crystals is adjusted by drying in a low-temperature oven.

REGION OF PRODUCTION:

EAST ANGLIA.

Medlar Jelly

DESCRIPTION:

FRUIT JELLIES ARE TRANSLUCENT, THEIR COLOURS VARY: MEDLARS YIELD A BRIGHT RED-BROWN, RED CURRANTS A RICH RUBY, QUINCES A RED-ORANGE, AND CHERRIES A DEEP DARK RED. MEDLAR IS A RELATIVELY ACID JELLY, WITH A SLIGHTLY WOODY AROMA. MOST MAKERS OF JELLIES NOW AIM FOR A HIGH FRUIT CONTENT WITH A SUGAR CONCENTRATION OF ABOUT 66 PER CENT.

HISTORY:

Recipes for medlar jelly, very similar to that now used, appear sporadically in British cookery texts from the early eighteenth century. Jellies based on fruit juices have always been popular with the British, if only as a means of preserving the crop; red currants, cherries, quinces and japonica (Japanese quince) are some of their favourite candidates. They owe their origin to European recipes such as that for quince paste (*marmelo*, the first stage of marmalade), popular in Renaissance Spain and Portugal (Wilson, 1973). They were made from many different types of fruit juice, boiled until concentrated enough to produce long-keeping, solid confections, stored in boxes and cut into slices for use. During the nineteenth century, different forms developed: one was the solid fruit jelly used as a sweetmeat, from which originated various children's sweets – the jellies, gums and pastilles now made on a vast scale – and the jellies made by housewives and jam companies as preserves. It is in the latter sector that one can still find artisan production of jellies based on unusual fruits. The southern part of East Anglia appears to be particularly rich in these products. It has relatively low rainfall and high summer temperatures, and is a good area for orchard and soft fruits of many types. Two of the country's largest jam companies, Tiptree (established by Wilkin & Sons in 1885) and Elsenham (1890) are located here, taking their names from their home towns in Essex.

TECHNIQUE:

Medlars need first to be chopped roughly. They are simmered with water and lemon juice until they become a pulp; the juice is extracted by draining it through a cloth without any pressure. The juice is measured and the appropriate amount of sugar added (normally reckoned to be about 675g per litre of juice). Once boiled to setting point, the jelly is potted, cooled and packed. Added pectin is not required.

REGION OF PRODUCTION:
EAST ANGLIA.

Sea Lavender Honey

DESCRIPTION:
THIS HONEY IS A PALE YELLOW-GREEN WHEN RUNNY, BUT GRANULATES RAPIDLY TO A HARD SET WITH A VERY SMOOTH TEXTURE. ITS FLAVOUR IS MILD BUT DISTINCT.

HISTORY:
Sea lavender is *Limonium vulgare*, a plant of the Statice family. This and several closely related species are natives, growing on mudflats around the coast of England and parts of southern Scotland. In places, especially Norfolk, it is a dominant species. According to F.N. Howes (1979), sea lavender was recognized in the 1930s or before as a bee-plant, producing light, good-quality honey.

The history of sea-lavender honey in East Anglia is essentially the effect on its habitat of man's attempts to protect the land. Much of the coast is made up of low-lying salt marshes, tidal creeks and mudflats. As long as records have been kept, there have been problems of erosion. A system of channels, dykes and sea walls has evolved to control the water levels which creates a larger area of suitable habitat for sea lavender than would naturally occur. Consequently, honey can be collected in economic quantities.

Bees have been kept for centuries in Britain, and sea-lavender honey has probably been collected, either alone or as part of a mixed flower honey, for as long as they have been present in East Anglia. The honey is not widely known, as the crop is small and almost all the production is consumed locally.

The hives are moved to the appropriate area at the start of the flowering season. Growing along tidal river channels between the high and low water marks, sea lavender flowers in August and good autumn weather promotes a large honey crop. The plant is a useful source of nectar at a time when the flowering season of most other species is over. Bees actively seek the plant, flying up to 1 km to work it. A few beekeepers collect the honey separately, have it analysed to establish the principal source and bottle it apart.

REGION OF PRODUCTION:
East Anglia.

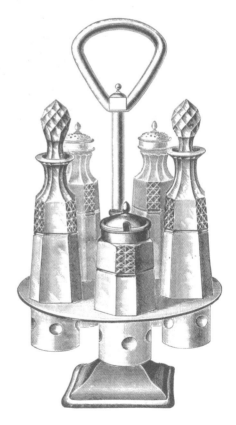

East Midlands

Good King Henry

DESCRIPTION:

GOOD KING HENRY IS A PLANT WHICH GROWS ABOUT 75CM HIGH, AND HAS LONG-STALKED, ARROW-SHAPED LEAVES. THE FLAVOUR IS LIKE SPINACH, ALTHOUGH IT BECOMES BITTER AS THE SEASON PROGRESSES.

HISTORY:

The plant *Chenopodium bonus-henricus* is known by many names: Blite, Lincolnshire Spinach, Wild Spinach, Allgood, Goosefoot and Mercury among them. This suggests that it has been known in Britain for a long time. There are plenty of archaeological remains that show it to have been part of Anglo-Saxon diet (Hagen, 1995). The name Good King Henry is derived originally from the German, *Guter Henrick*, a connection discussed by the herbalist John Gerard in 1636. John Evelyn (1699) said of English Mercury, 'or (as our country house-wives call it) all-good', that the young shoots could be eaten like asparagus, or it could later (i.e. the leaves) be boiled in a pottage.

With improved garden varieties of beet or spinach available at every turn, these semi-wild plants received scant notice in later works of kitchen wisdom. It was food for the poor, the gatherers of the countryside – in historical times, Scottish crofters turned to it for nourish-ment after the Clearances (MacNeill, 1929). However, the French gardener Vilmorin-Andrieux (1885) noticed that it was extensively grown by Lincolnshire farmers, 'almost every garden having its bed … Some say they like it better than asparagus,' and this comment has been echoed in general, without the Lincolnshire label, by subsequent authors (Rohde, 1943; Simon, 1960), who give the same culinary advice as John Evelyn.

In modern Britain, the use of Good King Henry for food is highly localized and does indeed occur principally in Lincolnshire. It is grown on a small scale by a few market gardeners, and sold on local produce stalls in central and north Lincolnshire. Local food specialist, Eileen Elder, says that it is boiled in plain water, or enclosed in a net and suspended in the broth whilst cooking bacon.

TECHNIQUE:

For the cultivation of Good King Henry, deep rich soil is best. Well-manured trenches about 60cm deep and 40cm apart are required; the plants are grown at intervals of about 30cm. The plant is a perennial and can also be found growing wild.

REGION OF PRODUCTION:

EAST MIDLANDS, LINCOLNSHIRE.

Seakale

DESCRIPTION:

SEAKALE HAS IVORY-COLOURED STALKS, SOMETIMES WITH A PURPLE TINGE; IN APPEARANCE THEY LOOK A LITTLE LIKE CELERY. THEY ARE PICKED WHEN ABOUT 23CM LONG. THE DIAMETER IS VARIABLE, RANGING FROM A FEW MILLIMETRES UP TO ABOUT 16MM. FLAVOUR: NUTTY, REMINISCENT OF CELERY BUT GENTLER.

HISTORY:

Wild sea kale, *Crambe maritima*, is native to the sea coasts of western Europe; as a garden plant, the English claim major responsibility for developing. It has been used as food in Britain since at least the seventeenth century, when John Evelyn (1699) wrote, 'our sea-keele … growing on our coast [is] very delicate'. The precise moment at which the vegetable entered the mainstream of British cookery is uncertain, but around this time the inhabitants of Kent, Sussex and Hampshire started to bleach the stems by banking them up with sand before cutting and taking them to market (Grigson, 1977). The plant was taken into cultivation at the end of the eighteenth century, and 'the popularity that it achieved in the eighteenth century is attributed to

Dr Lettsom of Camberwell, London' (MacCarthy, 1989). It was forced in beds of manure and straw to provide a fresh winter vegetable. Tall, bell-shaped terracotta pots were used to cover the plants and blanch the stalks. This was an expensive method of growing and led to a decline in the popularity of seakale towards the end of the century. Its cultivation was described in great detail by Vilmorin-Andrieux (1885), noting that it was very little used in France but much in England. Seakale can still be found growing wild in East Anglia but few plants are left because the passion for it during Victorian times stripped the coast almost bare when they were transported to gardens (Mabey, 1978).

Although seakale was widely cultivated at its height, it was always a luxury except in the areas to which it was native. In the first half of the twentieth century, a little seakale continued to be grown, mostly in private gardens, and the wild plants were harvested from the seashore.

TECHNIQUE:

The harvesting of wild seakale is now illegal on environmental grounds. About 30 years ago commercial production was recommenced by the Paske family in Lincolnshire. Because of the difficulty in obtaining plants, a strain was developed using seed collected from the Sussex coast. Propagation is continued by the use of thongs or root cuttings which are planted out in January. Deep, sandy, well-drained soil prepared by digging and manuring is best; the soils of Lincolnshire are well suited to this plant. They are allowed to grow for a season and then die back. Seakale is now grown in forcing sheds as a summer vegetable: the roots or crowns are lifted and stored in refrigerated conditions for a few weeks, then planted in heated sheds to produce the stems for cutting. Seakale must be blanched or it develops an acrid flavour, although Simon (1960) considered the taste of unblanched stalks to be much better developed.

REGION OF PRODUCTION:

EAST MIDLANDS, LINCOLNSHIRE.

Derby Cheese

DESCRIPTION:

HARD, PRESSED, PASTEURIZED COW'S MILK CHEESE MADE IN SMALL
WHEELS 30–34CM ACROSS AND 8–10CM DEEP, WEIGHING 14KG. COLOUR:
WHITE; SAGE DERBY IS MARBLED WITH GREEN JUICE. FLAVOUR AND
TEXTURE: CLEAN, MILD, SMOOTH.

HISTORY:

The history of Derby cheese is obscure. There are records as early as
1750 of its being carted to London for sale, but more precise
documentation is lacking (Black, 1989). It belongs to the same family
as Cheshire, and 'is one of the oldest British cheeses to become distinct
from the ancient widespread type once common to all the Midlands'
(Rance, 1982). The recipes were kept secret and many forgotten.
Derby cheese was the first to be made in a creamery, in 1870. Some
farmhouse cheese-making survived in South Derbyshire until 1930s.
The local agricultural college at Sutton Bonnington was responsible
for introducing standards.

Historically, the sage-flavoured cheeses were produced in spring to
be eaten in the autumn. Sage juice was used for flavour, and the juices
of some other leaf, such as spinach, for colour. White and coloured
curd were made separately and used for alternate layers in the mould.

TECHNIQUE:

The milk is heated to a temperature of 21°C and 1.5 per cent starter
added. The temperature is raised to about 28°C and the acidity allowed
to develop to the correct level, at which point rennet is added and the
surface of the milk gently stirred until it begins to coagulate. About 45
minutes after coagulation the curd is cut into 1cm cubes, and allowed
to settle for a few minutes. The curd (which is rather fragile) is stirred
carefully whilst the temperature is raised to 34°C over a period of
about 50 minutes. The curd is allowed to settle until the acidity is
correct, after which it is drained quickly, cut into blocks, and piled
down the sides of the vat. The process of cutting and turning continues
until the correct acidity is achieved. The curd is put though a coarse

mill, mixed with the salt, and then packed into moulds lined with coarse cloths. The cheeses are pressed until the whey runs freely; pressing continues for 24 hours, the cheeses being removed and turned once. They are capped and bandaged or waxed. Ripening is at 12°C. The cheeses are turned daily. The technique for making Sage Derby is identical until moulding when colouring and flavouring are added to the curd.

REGION OF PRODUCTION:
EAST MIDLANDS.

Leicester Cheese

DESCRIPTION:
A PRESSED COW'S MILK CHEESE IN LARGE, SHALLOW WHEELS 40CM ACROSS AND 8CM DEEP; OR IN RECTANGULAR BLOCKS. COLOUR: DEEP ORANGE-RED. FLAVOUR AND TEXTURE: SWEETISH, SLIGHTLY CARAMEL; FLAKY.

HISTORY:
Leicestershire has contributed 2 great cheeses to the British repertoire. One, Stilton, is famous; the other, Leicester, is less well known yet probably has as long a history. Both owe their celebrity to the rich pasture lands around Melton Mowbray.

Leicester had become a distinct variety before the eighteenth century. The southern half of the county was known for its large, hard, red cheeses. Rance (1982) speculates the makers were influenced by Gloucestershire methods, citing similarities in technique. Much of the production was consumed in towns nearby. This remained true until 1939–45 for, Burdett (1935) says, Leicester was not well known in London.

Wartime circumstances affected production through the banning of annatto – used in large amounts to produce the deep red considered a part of the character (it is often called Red Leicester). Although the cheese continued to be made through the war, the pale, undyed version upset many consumers. Experts of today would have agreed with their distress. Rance states that the dye contributes to the visual assessment of quality as it is mottled in a badly-produced cheese. He also claims it enhances flavour. Most Leicester is now factory made.

TECHNIQUE:

Craft and creamery methods are similar. The milk is heated to 21°C and the starter (about 2 per cent) mixed through; annatto is added and the milk stirred thoroughly. The temperature is raised to 29°C and rennet added when the correct acidity is reached; the surface is stirred to prevent the cream separating. The curd is cut several times until the particles are the size of wheat grains. The curd is stirred and the heat raised to 33–34°C over 40 minutes; then it is allowed to settle until the correct acidity is reached. The whey is drained by pressing the curd under weighted wooden racks, after which it is cut into blocks and stacked at either side of the vat. The blocks are cut and repiled until the acidity is correct. The curd is finely ground in a Cheshire-type mill, and salt is added (about 1kg to 45kg curd). Moulding is into the characteristic shallow hoop, lined with a much lighter cheese-cloth than generally used in Britain. It is pressed for 2 days, the cheeses turned twice into clean cloths. Maturing takes 6–9 months. Traditionally, the cloth was removed for the last 2 weeks of ripening to allow the crust to blue.

REGION OF PRODUCTION:

EAST MIDLANDS.

Stilton Cheese

DESCRIPTION:

PASTEURIZED COW'S MILK CHEESE. WEIGHTS ARE 2.5–5.7KG; SMALL STILTONS, ABOUT 500G, ARE ALSO PRODUCED. THE SHAPE IS A TALL CYLINDER. A BLUE STILTON SHOULD HAVE AN UNCRACKED, TOUGH, HARD CRUST, SLIGHTLY IRREGULAR, PALE BROWN-GREY IN COLOUR, WITH POWDERY WHITE PATCHES. THE INTERIOR VARIES FROM CREAM TO PALE

YELLOW, DEPENDING ON THE MAKER, SHADING DARKER TOWARDS THE RIND, WITH EXTENSIVE, WELL-SPREAD, GREEN-BLUE VEINING; TEXTURES RANGE FROM CRUMBLING TO SMOOTH, SOFT TO FIRM. WHITE STILTON IS VERY PALE. THE CHEESE SOFTENS AS IT BLUES, AND BLUE STILTON IS CREAMY AND MELLOW. THE BEST EXAMPLES HAVE AN INTENSE, WINY FLAVOUR. WHITE STILTON HAS A SHARP FLAVOUR.

HISTORY:

Unlike other British territorial cheeses, it was named for the place where it was sold, rather than the area where it was made. It originated around Melton Mowbray, on the borders of Leicester, Rutland and Nottingham. Quality cheese was known in the district at least as early as the reign of Queen Anne (d. 1714). The first Stilton was probably white and high-fat, but with a natural tendency to blue. The excellent flavour produced when this happened meant it became famous as a blue-vein cheese. It gained its reputation when it was sold at the Bell Inn in Stilton, Huntingdonshire, in the first quarter of the eighteenth century. This was a coaching house on the main route north from London. By the time Daniel Defoe passed through in 1722, he was able to write that Stilton was a town 'famous for cheese, which is called our English Parmesan, and is brought to the table with the mites or maggots around it, so thick, that they bring a spoon with them for you to eat the mites with, as you do the cheese'. Another enthusiast of Stilton, though with reservations, was the botanist Richard Bradley (1736). He claimed that its rennet was flavoured with plenty of mace, and that 'without the people of Stilton keep up the antient way of making it, agreeable to the old Receipt, they must of necessity lose the Reputation they have gained … I shall not pretend to affirm why the Cheeses now in that town are not generally so good as they were formerly; but perhaps it is because the Cheese-sellers there … now buy Cheeses from other parts, where nothing of the true Receipt is known.' By the end of that century, the cheese was widely made round Melton Mowbray, and in many villages of Rutland. It was supplied to nearby innkeepers, who sold it to their

often well-heeled customers who were in the country to hunt (see Melton Mowbray pork pie, p.59).

Creamery Stilton was first produced in the 1870s, but it remained quite different from the farmhouse cheese. The makers were very secretive and it was not until early in the 1900s, when they formed an association, that recipes came into the public domain. (Although one had in fact been published several times in the 1720s by Richard Bradley.) The making of Stilton extended by that time as far as Hartington in Dovedale (Derbyshire) but never any further. The makers, aware of the damage done to other British cheeses by copies made outside the area of origin, sought legal protection for their product. Stilton was defined by them in 1910, and given a protected name under a High Court judgement of 1969 which stated: 'Stilton is a blue or white cheese made from full cream milk, with no applied pressure, forming its own crust or coat and made in cylindrical form, the milk coming from English dairy herds in the district of Melton Mowbray and the surrounding areas falling within the counties of Leicestershire (now including Rutland), Derbyshire and Nottinghamshire.' This has prevented the development of block cheeses and imitations. Both blue and white Stilton have been awarded Protected Designations of Origin.

TECHNIQUE:

All Stilton is manufactured in creameries using pasteurized milk. The methods vary in detail. After pasteurization, the milk is cooled to a temperature of about 30°C and starter is added, followed by rennet. After 60–90 minutes, the curd is cut and allowed to settle. The whey is drawn off over 1–4 hours until the curd has shrunk by half. When the correct acidity is achieved, the curd is scooped on to a long, perforated metal tray or 'Stilton sink'. Providing the acidity develops correctly, the curd is cut into blocks 4.5cm square after the first hour and then turned. Cutting and turning continue until the correct acidity is reached. The curd is milled coarsely to give pieces the size of walnuts. The curd is divided into batches sufficient for each cheese and salt mixed through (30g to 1.5kg curd). It is then scooped into a Stilton hoop (a perforated metal cylinder 30cm deep and 18cm diameter). These are drained 4–10 days at 15°C, turned daily. They are injected with mould spores. On removal of the hoop, the cheeses are scraped, the scrapings used to seal any cracks or holes. The cheeses are stored in a cool, damp room until a coat is formed. They are ripened at 10°C in a relative humidity of 94–98 per cent. After 4 weeks the cheese is pierced with skewers to admit air and speed the growth of mould. Each cheese is turned daily and brushed to prevent mite infestation.

White Stilton is based on a drier, less acid curd, and is eaten at about the age of 20 days.

REGION OF PRODUCTION:
EAST MIDLANDS.

Faggot

DESCRIPTION:
ROUGHLY SPHERICAL RISSOLES OF COOKED PORK AND OFFAL WRAPPED IN CAUL FAT OR COATED IN CRUMBS, 6–8CM DIAMETER, WEIGHING 100–150G. COLOUR: GREYISH-BROWN, WITH A PALE LACE PATTERN FROM A WRAPPING OF CAUL FAT; ALTERNATIVELY, THEY MAY BE SPRINKLED WITH BREAD CRUMBS (ESPECIALLY THE NORTHERN VERSIONS). FLAVOUR: MEATY, TENDING TOWARDS LIVER, WITH ONIONS, SPICES AND HERBS, SAGE THE MOST COMMON.

HISTORY:
Faggots (the word means a bundle) are really a primitive type of sausage, collections of finely chopped pork offal held together by squares of caul fat as opposed to skins. Originally, they provided a way for using the less attractive parts of a pig such as the pluck. An early use of the word is found in Mayhew (1851) and, a few years later, the faggot is dismissed as a product of 'cheap pork butchery' (*OED*), but such dishes must have been known long before that and have been

quite widespread. Sometimes, they also seem to be called haslet, see below. Wright (1896–1905) cites mentions from counties in the East and West Midlands and the South from Sussex to Somerset. Versions are also known in Wales as Welsh faggots, where the recipe diverges from that of the Midlands by using oats instead of bread crumbs, and sometimes the addition of apple pieces, alongside the chopped or minced offal and pork. Bog myrtle (*Myrica Gale*) was a seasoning in Wales, although now little used (Mabey, 1978).

In Yorkshire and Lancashire a similar dish is known as savoury duck. This is sometimes presented as a loaf from which chunks are cut, rather than as rissoles. It tends to have a higher cereal content and is blander in flavour. It sounds very like a method of getting rid of all the scraps in a pork-butcher's. Instructions for making savoury ducks (Finney, 1915) read: 'To make Savoury Ducks (sometimes called Spice Balls), take all the odds and ends, such as Puddings, Sausages, Brawn, Ends of Bacon, or whatever may be left over, boil for a short time, chop fine and season ... Pack into roasting tins, and place in a good sharp oven until the fat commences to boil out of them. If not allowed to boil as stated, they invariably turn sour in a short time.'

In all areas where such items are popular, they can be seen displayed on trays in the windows of butchers' shops, especially those who specialize in pork products. In some places, butchers sell a mixture of raw faggot meat for home cooks to use in their own versions. Faggots can be eaten cold but are more usually heated. They are often served with peas: opinions vary as to whether this should be a dish of green peas or a purée of dried ones. As faggots would originally have been a winter dish made at pig-killing time, dried peas are probably what was expected. Savoury duck is sometimes sliced and fried.

TECHNIQUE:

A mixture of pork offal – liver, lungs, spleen – and fat, bread crumbs, onions and flavourings is chopped or minced finely and then parcelled in squares of caul (the fatty membrane which wraps and suspends the various organs in the abdomen). Odds and ends of lean pork and meat products such as ham are added by some butchers. In some places, the mixture is simply pressed into a tray and baked. The parcels are packed into a tin and baked at 180°C for 40–60 minutes. They are reheated at home.

REGION OF PRODUCTION:
MIDLANDS; SOUTH ENGLAND; WALES.

Haslet

DESCRIPTION:
COOKED, BRINED PORK AND OFFAL IN LONG OBLONG LOAVES 10–15CM WIDE, 6–8CM DEEP; IT IS CUT THINLY TO GIVE SLICES 3–4 MM THICK, WEIGHING ABOUT 30G. COLOUR: BEIGE-PINK WITH SPECKS OF WHITE AND DEEPER PINK; SOMETIMES SPECKLED WITH HERBS; WITH A DARK BROWN EDGE ON THE SIDE EXPOSED TO HEAT IN COOKING. FLAVOUR: BRINED PORK, SEASONINGS (USUALLY BLACK PEPPER AND SOMETIMES SAGE).

HISTORY:
Haslet is often treated as a dialect word, although Wright (1896–1905) places it in Lincolnshire and Cheshire and most counties directly south, as far as the Isle of Wight, which makes it quite a non-regional dialect. The food, however, does have a regional ring – Lincolnshire is the county linked most closely. The word itself (found as harslet, hazelet or acelet) is derived from an Old French root that relates both to spits and the meat roasted on them. By the time Cotgrave wrote his French–English dictionary in 1611, the French had particularized some of the original meaning onto offal and innards that might be spitted and roasted (*OED*). So, too, had the English, connecting it especially (but not invariably) to the pig, rather as they had the once more general words bacon and brawn. This was the sense in which Pepys and Hannah Glasse used haslet, as it was the farmers' wives of Northamptonshire who sent pies filled with haslet as presents to neighbours at pig-killing time. Eliza Acton (1845) describes 'harslet' pudding, containing 'the heart, liver, kidneys &c of the pig',

which she says was held in much esteem in certain counties. By transference, it came to describe the very dish itself, made from the pluck by chopping and roasting or boiling the pieces. In Lincolnshire, haslet was closely related to faggots or sausages, and Maria Rundell (1807) seems also to describe a faggot, but she calls it haslet, when she instructs her readers to enclose a mixture of offal, scraps of lean pork and some onion in caul, sew it up and roast it.

Haslet nowadays means a kind of meat loaf, made of finely chopped odds and ends of lean and cured pork, highly seasoned, and baked until brown on top. It is usually sliced and eaten cold with salad for dinner or high tea. It is widely produced by craft butchers, particularly in Lincolnshire but also throughout southern England.

TECHNIQUE:

The meat is minced or finely ground and mixed with seasonings, often with a proportion of cereal; the mixture is packed into dishes then baked at about 180°C for 60 minutes.

REGION OF PRODUCTION:

EAST MIDLANDS, LINCOLNSHIRE; SOUTH ENGLAND.

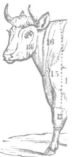

Lincoln Red Cattle

DESCRIPTION:

A YOUNG HEIFER YIELDS 220–250KG; A 2-YEAR-OLD ANIMAL GIVES 300–350KG; GOOD CONFORMATION WITH LONG HINDQUARTERS. FLAVOUR EXCELLENT, ESPECIALLY OLDER ANIMALS; WHEN FATTENED, THE FLESH IS WELL MARBLED.

HISTORY:

Lincoln Red cattle (so-called because of their dark, ginger-maroon pelts) were developed in the nineteenth century out of the classic Victorian beef breed, the Shorthorn. This was interbred with the local red cattle to give a slow-growing, hardy animal which could live on the poor grasslands of the Wolds, an area of rolling country which stretches from the Humber southwards to East Anglia. In fact, in the

W ho would think that an Australian would consider the Lincoln Red as one of the best types of beef cattle in the world? Worryingly, it is now on the endangered list distributed by the Rare Breed Society Trust, the guardians of pure-breed British cattle, sheep, pork and poultry.

Rich in flavour with well-formed textural meat, these cattle are hard to come by but deliver at the highest order. Beef with heritage has always been my personal choice, as I wholly believe in true provenance. Traceability is just a made-up word to cover intensive farming and shortcuts in farming practices.

The Lincoln is quality beef that should be served with reverence, the loin left on the bone to mature for at least twenty-four days and as long as sixty days. (At sixty days the flavour changes from a rich butter to a mature cheese with veins of blue.) It should be butchered into thick steak, the fore-rib left on the bone, seasoned well and brushed with the smallest amount of oil. Place the steak over glowing coals, cook it rare and set it to one side to rest for five minutes before serving it with fresh horseradish spiced with a squeeze of lemon and bound with the smallest amount of fresh cream.

John Torode

CHEF, SMITHS OF SMITHFIELD, LONDON

seventeenth century, Gervase Markham had praised Lincolnshire 'pied' cattle – not red – but had none the less thought the county top-notch for fine bloodstock. Early this century, Lincoln Reds were reckoned the largest of the British beef breeds. Modern imperatives demand lean, fast-maturing beef animals: they have done no favours to the slower Lincoln, with a tendency to put on fat when generously fed. Extensively farmed cattle are leaner. Polled Lincoln Reds are a variant, bred from bloodlines without horns.

TECHNIQUE:

Lincoln Reds were developed to be docile and good mothers. They can thrive on sparse vege-tation; they grazed the marginal grassland on the dry, chalky soils of the Wolds. A few herds still exist in this way. In the past, they were kept for several years for breeding before being slaughtered for beef, a custom which produced very well-flavoured meat. However, many are now raised on mixed farms which grow barley for winter fodder. The herds calve in spring or autumn; spring is currently more favoured. The calves are suckled until weaning, then finished for market. They are killed rather young, at 12–18 months. For commercial herds, continental European breeds are now much favoured for crossing, particularly the Limousin and the Belgian Blue. However, pure-bred Lincoln beef still has its supporters, and some butchers in their home region specialize in it.

REGION OF PRODUCTION:

EAST ENGLAND, LINCOLNSHIRE.

Lincolnshire Sausages

DESCRIPTION:

AN UNCOOKED, FRESH PORK SAUSAGE 12CM LONG, 2–2.5CM DIAMETER. WEIGHT: USUALLY 8 TO THE POUND (450G). COLOUR: PALE PINK, MOTTLED WITH DEEPER RED, AND GREEN FLECKS. FLAVOUR: A RICH, MEATY PORK FLAVOUR, WITH DISTINCT TASTE OF SAGE.

HISTORY:

Lincolnshire has relied on the pig more than most for meat and fat. A famous nineteenth-century breed (now sadly extinct), the Lincolnshire Curly Coat, developed here. Country people kept pigs and preserved their meat for the family. Sausages in the British tradition (fresh lean and fat pork, bread or rusk, and seasonings) were made by everyone at pig-killing time. The breed of pig used has been affected, as have all other pork products, by the development of modern hybrids and the demand for lean meat.

It is not clear how long Lincolnshire sausages have been thought noteworthy; only that the tradition of pork butchery has been in existence for centuries. Neil Curtis, whose family have been pork butchers in the city of Lincoln since 1828, remarks that the sausages are made with meat more coarsely chopped than that used elsewhere. Dalton (*c.* 1930) noted in his compilation of butchers' recipes that use of coarsely chopped meat is a distinctly northern preference. The addition of sage is essential to the modern Lincoln sausage seasoning. This is paralleled by the Lincolnshire pork pie seasoning, recorded as demanding sage (Finney, 1915).

A strong base of small butchers, plus a handful of larger firms, still produce good Lincolnshire sausages throughout the county and surrounding areas. Elsewhere, the designation 'Lincolnshire' is sometimes used for a premium quality, herb-seasoned sausage.

TECHNIQUE:

The pork is selected in the correct proportions of fat and lean; it is coarsely chopped or ground, combined with bread crumbs or rusk, plus a little iced water, and seasoned – always with sage and salt, other spices to taste. Some makers add preservative. The meat is filled into casings; natural casings made from the small intestines of the hog (bacon pig) are the usual choice, although sheep's small intestines may be used for chipolatas.

REGION OF PRODUCTION:

EAST MIDLANDS, LINCOLNSHIRE.

Lincolnshire Stuffed Chine

DESCRIPTION:

STUFFED CHINE IS MADE FROM THE UNSPLIT BACKBONE OF A BACON PIG; THE SMALLEST PIECE WHICH IS PRACTICABLE WEIGHS ABOUT 2.5KG. WHOLE CHINES AVERAGE 7–8KG, AND MAY WEIGH UP TO 15KG. THE JOINT IS SQUARISH-OBLONG IN SHAPE. COLOUR: THE MEAT IS A DEEP PINK-RED WITH WHITE FAT ON THE SKIN SIDE; THE STUFFING IS DARK GREEN, AND WHEN CORRECTLY CARVED, THE SLICES ARE STRIPED RED AND GREEN IN NARROW BARS. FLAVOUR: THE MEAT RESEMBLES BACON; THE STUFFING HAS A MILD PARSLEY FLAVOUR, WITH A HAY-LIKE AROMA.

HISTORY:

Chine is an old English word for backbone, derived from Norman French. It was in general culinary use to indicate the backbone, with some attached flesh, of any animal, both fish and meat, until the eighteenth century. It continued to be used in connection with bacon pigs – from which the sides are normally removed without splitting the backbone. This progressive narrowing of a word's meaning from all species to the pig alone is a tendency already noticed with bacon, brawn and haslet.

It is not apparent when the Lincolnshire version of stuffed chine developed, but it is a county in which pig rearing has always been important, and oral tradition states the dish has a long history. When the French poet Verlaine was schoolmastering in the south Lincolnshire town of Boston, he fell in love with chine – so much so that he tried, and failed, to find it elsewhere in Britain (Grigson, 1984). The chine is preserved by salting until required, and then made up by slashing the meat and stuffing it with chopped herbs. Webb (*c.* 1930) noted that the stuffings varied, some households using only chopped parsley, and others relying on a mixture of herbs including lettuce leaves, young nettles, thyme, marjoram, sage and black currant leaves.

Customarily, the chine was reserved for special occasions, including christenings and May hiring fairs (at which farm workers returned to

their homes). It is still more popular at certain times of the year, in May and at Christmas, and at the local agricultural shows.

TECHNIQUE:

The pig forequarter is butchered to give the spine with some muscle still attached on either side. The meat is wet-cured in a mixture of salt, saltpetre, sugar, black treacle, beer and spices for 2 weeks, followed by 1 week's dry cure in salt. The meat is slashed at right angles to the spine and stuffed with chopped parsley or a mixture of herbs. At this stage the joint is ready to be cooked. It is immersed in simmering water for up to 7 hours (depending on size); the meat should be enclosed in a huff paste, a cloth, or, more commonly today, a roasting bag. Once removed from the pot, the meat is drained, cooled and carved in thin slices, parallel to the bone.

REGION OF PRODUCTION:

EAST MIDLANDS, CENTRAL LINCOLNSHIRE.

Melton Mowbray Pork Pie

DESCRIPTION:

A COOKED, RAISED PIE FILLED WITH PORK. COLOUR: DEEP GOLD BROWN PASTRY CRUST; A FILLING OF COARSELY CHOPPED UNCURED PORK, MARBLED GREYISH-PINK AND WHITE, WITH A THIN LAYER OF PALE OPAQUE JELLY BETWEEN THE MEAT AND PASTRY. FLAVOUR: PORK FLAVOUR, HIGHLY SEASONED WITH PEPPER; CRUNCHY PASTRY.

HISTORY:

The raised or standing pie, of which this is an example, developed from the medieval and Elizabethan habit of making pastry cases, or coffins, from a very robust paste. These could be filled and baked without any support from a mould. Originally they were made simply from water and flour and were only intended to contain and protect the meat during baking: they were thrown away, not eaten. It is from this tradition, not from simple dish pies covered with pastry, that modern pork pies descend.

There are 2 reasons why those of Melton Mowbray in Leicestershire probably achieved fame, says Stephen Hallam, who makes them. Firstly, from at least the 1700s, the area supported a substantial cheese-making industry, producing surplus whey to feed large herds of pigs. Secondly, the town was headquarters of aristocratic hunts. Pork pies were the ideal picnic for hungry sportsmen who came to follow the fox hounds.

How long the pies have been recognized is not clear, perhaps no longer than 150 years (Mabey, 1978). The firm of Dickinson and Morris was founded in the mid-nineteenth century and it is now only Dickinson and Morris's Ye Olde Pork Pie Shoppe that claims to make pies to the original specification. At the end of the 1800s, the pies were available by post from Tebutt's, another local manufacturer, who had 'an unsullied reputation extending over thirty years' (Law, *c.* 1895).

Consumer perception of Melton Mowbray pork pies is nowadays confused. People from outside the area perceive them as a premium pie of the standard English type. They certainly fit the bill, having particular qualities that aficionados desire: the 'baggy' shape, rich crunchy pastry, and coarsely chopped fresh pork (not brined as are generic pork pies – see below), with a good seasoning of black pepper.

TECHNIQUE:

A hot-water crust is used. Lard, water and salt are boiled and mixed into flour. Whilst still hot, the crust is moulded by hand around a 'dolly', or cylindrical wooden block later removed to leave space for the filling. This is hand-chopped, lean, uncured pork with salt and a little fat. A circle of pastry is placed over the top of the filled pie, sealed and egg-washed. Pies are baked at 210°C for 30 minutes, then at 160°C for 1–2 hours. Once baked, a stock from pigs' feet and bones is poured in through a hole in the top. This must be at the right temperature: too hot and the crust absorbs the stock and softens. The whole is cooled; the stock jellies.

REGION OF PRODUCTION:

EAST MIDLANDS, MELTON MOWBRAY (LEICESTERSHIRE).

'Let the stoics say what they please, we do not eat for the good of living, but because the meat is savory and the appetite is keen.'
RALPH WALDO EMERSON

Pork Pie

DESCRIPTION:

COOKED RAISED PIES OF BRINED PORK; INDIVIDUAL ONES WEIGHING ABOUT 150G ARE APPROXIMATELY 7CM DIAMETER, 4–5CM DEEP; LARGER PIES ARE MADE IN WEIGHTS OF 250–1000G. FORM: CIRCULAR, WITH CRIMPED EDGES, OFTEN DECORATED WITH PASTRY LEAVES. THE PIES ARE ALWAYS DEEP IN PROPORTION TO THEIR HEIGHT, AND MAY BE STRAIGHT-SIDED (IF MADE IN A MOULD) OR SLIGHTLY IRREGULAR AND BAGGY IF HAND-RAISED. COLOUR: EXTERIOR IS A DEEP GOLD-BROWN PASTRY WITH A SHINY TOP; WHEN CUT, THE PASTRY IS WHITE INSIDE, WITH A LAYER OF CLEAR JELLY BETWEEN IT AND A FILLING OF PORK, WHICH IS USUALLY BRINED AND A DEEP ROSE-PINK. FLAVOUR: RICH SALTED PORK FLAVOUR, OFTEN HIGHLY SEASONED WITH PEPPER, PLUS VERY CRISP PASTRY.

HISTORY:

The stronghold of the pork pie is the Midlands, although they are popular, widely marketed and made, to a lesser extent, in other parts. There is a noticeable trend away from pork as one progresses through the far north of England into Scotland, where beef and lamb are more common in meat products, including pies.

Farmers and yeomen, or even cottagers, might make them at pig-killing time, after putting the main joints down to bacon and ham. Great lords might eat them at any time: Henry de Lacy, Earl of Lincoln, had his kitchen buy a shilling's worth of pork 'pro pastillis' – for pies – in 1299 (Woolgar, 1992). Today, however, they are more likely part of the special range of products associated with pork butchers. Until recently, most large towns had at least one of these. From this base of artisanal knowledge several large companies have developed. In the view of many, pork pies were a useful way of using up scraps left over after the pig had been butchered for fresh meat, hams or bacon. The bones contributed the savoury jelly and the flesh was an economical by-product.

It is curious that both pork pies and pork butchers have little detectable history before the nineteenth century. The social historian Robert Roberts who wrote an account of his early life in Salford at the beginning of the last century (Roberts, 1971), makes the observation that one consequence of the introduction of compulsory military service in a united Germany after 1871 was emigration, particularly of Bavarians. Many of them settled in Britain, often in the wake of richer settlers involved in the cotton and wool trades of Manchester and Bradford. Among this second wave were many pork butchers – themselves well versed in their trade and anxious to extend the meagre British range compared to the variety and ingenuity of German products. 'By the outbreak of the First World War it is doubtful if there was a single Northern town, large or small, that did not have its German pork butchers. Each one ... introduced a range of new tastes to the British working class.'

They did not need to invent the pork pie, for pies in general were well-known. This included large raised 'standing pies' composed of meat fillings in a hot-water crust. Pork pies share a common heritage with other English raised pies such as the Melton Mowbray (filled with unbrined pork, see above) and game pies, in that the pastry probably originated as a simple flour and water mixture intended to contain and protect the meat. Dorothy Hartley (1954) gives a fourteenth-century recipe for a 'pig pye' (probably indicating a sucking pig at this date). She discusses variants on seasonings, fillings and decorations used in the Midland counties of England, most of which are now rarely encountered outside domestic kitchens. Many have disappeared as the country habit of killing pigs on farms has been eroded by advances in food preservation, changes in shopping habits, and the tightening of regulations relating to slaughter and meat handling.

Few literary paeans to the pork pie can be as eloquent as Rebecca West's in her novel *The Fountain Overflows* (1957): 'Aunt Lily … paused to tell us that whereas there were a great many good butchers, ordinary butchers, a good pork butcher was as rare as an archbishop.' This is preface to an account of buying the ingredients (including the best black peppercorns and the whitest lard), magically raising the crust (to use a mould was 'a mug's game'), and producing the finished article. 'Queenie would never let the children eat anything vulgar,' is the epilogue, 'Harry liked it, when he went out in his boat.'

Aunt Lily's pork pie contained hard-boiled egg – by no means an invariable component, but long, loaf-shaped pork pies with hard-boiled eggs running through the middle are also made. This arrangement is also seen in the veal-and-ham pie.

TECHNIQUE:

Pork pies differ over minor points to do with shape and seasoning between makers and regions. For the pastry, they require a hot-water crust, made by heating water and lard to boiling point, stirring it into the flour and kneading; this produces a dough that is malleable whilst hot but which sets firm when cold. This is important when the pies are raised by hand: the warm pastry is shaped over a wooden dolly or cylindrical mould which is removed to leave a deep case which holds the shape without support. However, many butchers and large pie companies use tin moulds in which the pies remain during baking. For very special occasions, elaborately moulded and fluted tins may be used. The filling is always composed of a mixture of lean and fat pork, usually (but not invariably) brined, turning the meat a characteristic pink. The texture of the filling is generally fairly solid, the pork being minced coarsely. Pepper is the favoured seasoning; other spices, such as ginger and nutmeg, may also be added. The pork butcher Thomas Finney (1915) listed seasonings for Nottingham, Liverpool, Yorkshire, Manchester and Lincolnshire: distinguished by the inclusion of mace, cinnamon, nutmeg, coriander, and ginger respectively. A portion of meat is placed in the case, covered with a pastry lid, and the edges crimped together; a small hole is cut in the centre of the lid; in the past, this was often covered with a pastry rose, and the top of the pies decorated with pastry leaves and flowers. Pies are baked at 230°C for 45 minutes or longer, depending on size. After baking, the hot pies are filled with a strong gelatinous stock which sets to become a clear jelly on cooling.

The best pies are generally made by pork butchers, and hand-raising shows care and attention to detail, although perfectly good pies are made in tins. In Lincolnshire, the pie was a customary treat for breakfast at Christmas. They are found in all regions, even if their epicentre is the Midlands, and are consumed by the million as a snack or as part of a summer salad meal.

REGION OF PRODUCTION:
MIDLANDS.

Spiced Beef

DESCRIPTION:
COOKED, SPICED AND CURED BEEF, SOLD SLICED OR IN JOINTS OF 2.5–3KG. COLOUR: THE OUTSIDE IS DEEP BROWN, THE INSIDE BROWNISH PINK. FLAVOUR: A GOOD BEEF TASTE, SALTY, WITH PEPPER AND SPICES.

HISTORY:
For many centuries, beef was preserved by salting. Spiced beef is a development of this. In most surviving recipes it is dry-salted, the meat being kept in pickle for 10–21 days and then smoked or cooked. The beef kept well after cooking; up to 3 weeks is generally quoted. This was a virtue, especially when numbers at table were unpredictable. Kitchiner (1817) remarked that the dish deserved 'the particular attention of those families who frequently have Accidental Customers dropping in at Luncheon or Supper'. David (1970) remarks that it was a regular Christmas dish in many English country houses and farms, and that it has been known for at least 300 years under various names. There is a persistent association between this

dish and hunting; it is often called hunting or huntsman's beef and would have sat well on the sideboard at a hunt breakfast. Melton Hunt beef, made in huge pieces up to 15kg at a time, was one of the best-known recipes. It is now more likely to be centrepiece of a buffet and is mostly made at Christmas.

TECHNIQUE:

Although numerous recipes for spiced beef, huntsman's beef and variations with regional names attached can be found, the principles and ingredients are all similar. The cuts are round or topside; brisket can also be used. The piece should weigh about 3kg; it can be larger, in which case curing time will be longer, but it should not be smaller. The beef is rubbed with the curing mixture – the producer located for this study includes black treacle, mace, allspice and garlic in the mix; other recipes require salt, saltpetre, and brown sugar and crushed spices – black peppercorns, allspice, juniper berries and bay leaves are often used. Nutmeg and cloves are sometimes used instead of the allspice and juniper; shallots and garlic were used in Melton Hunt beef. The meat marinates in this, being turned and rubbed every day for up to 2 weeks, depending on the size of the joint. Once removed from the pickle, the meat is cooked on a very low heat for about 5 hours in a close-fitting pot half-filled with water, sealed with greaseproof paper or a flour and water crust. The joint is removed from the cooking liquor, wrapped in greaseproof paper and pressed under a small weight until absolutely cold.

REGION OF PRODUCTION:
MIDLANDS; SOUTH-WEST ENGLAND.

Ashbourne Gingerbread

DESCRIPTION:

EACH PIECE HAS A DOMED PROFILE; THE BASE IS AN ELONGATED HEXAGON. ON THE TOP, THE MARK RESULTING FROM SLICING THE DOUGH, WHICH HAS THEN RISEN A LITTLE, GIVES A SIMPLE BUT DECORATIVE PATTERN OF LINES. THEY MEASURE APPROXIMATELY

65MM BY 55MM BY 15MM HIGH. WEIGHT: 25G. COLOUR: PALE GOLD TO DEEP CREAM ON OUTSIDE, CREAMY YELLOW OPEN CRUMB INSIDE, WITH SMALL LENGTHWAYS CRACKS. FLAVOUR AND TEXTURE: SWEET, MILD GINGER FLAVOUR, WITH CANDIED PEEL GIVING A BITTER ORANGE NOTE; CRISP, BISCUIT TEXTURE.

HISTORY:

So many of the cakes and pies that have survived in British towns and villages are in some sense or other fairings, made for a high day or holiday. Presumably, 'Ashbourne' was a fairing too, fixed for perpetuity by the town being a centre for tourism in the Peak district (tourism seems to act as stimulus and preservative for local foods) as well as by the existence of a long-lasting commercial baker – in this case the firm of Spencer. Spencer's claims that this gingerbread dates from at least the 1820s. The estimate seems conservative. Since then, several other companies have been started by members of the Spencer family or people who have worked for them.

Ashbourne gingerbread always seems to have been pale in colour but, unlike that once known in Grantham (Lincolnshire), never to have contained eggs. The recipes which are available show it to be similar to shortbread. The texture and the addition of candied peel (also found in some other British gingerbreads) indicate a long history, perhaps with an origin in the buttery, unleavened shortcakes of the seventeenth century rather than the stiff, dark, spiced confections of flour and treacle then known as gingerbread.

TECHNIQUE:

The exact method is a trade secret. The ingredients are given as flour, sugar, margarine, eggs, butter, ground ginger, citrus peel, raising agents, salt. Published recipes call for flour, butter and caster sugar in the approximate proportions 4:3:2. The butter and sugar are creamed together and mixed to a dough with flour, powdered ginger and chopped candied lemon peel. It is fashioned into a roll about 20mm thick which is cut into 40mm lengths. It is baked at 180°C for 20 minutes. The gingerbread should remain very pale.

Grantham Gingerbread

DESCRIPTION:

HOLLOW, SLIGHTLY DOME-SHAPED BISCUITS, ABOUT 50MM DIAMETER.
COLOUR: PALE GOLD. FLAVOUR AND TEXTURE: SWEET AND GINGERY,
WITH AN OPEN HONEYCOMB CENTRE WHICH IS CRISP BUT DISSOLVES
EASILY IN THE MOUTH.

HISTORY:

This belongs to a family of hard, pale gingerbread biscuits made in the
East Midlands. An early reference to a Grantham biscuit is in the diary
of the seventeenth-century antiquary Ralph Thoresby who noted a
peculiar sort of thin cake known as Grantham whetstones (Pointer,
1980). No-one knows exactly what these were; an eighteenth-century
recipe for whetstone cakes from neighbouring Leicestershire shows a
flour, sugar and egg biscuit spiced with caraway and rose water. The
relationship between these and Grantham gingerbreads is not clear. The
'invention' of the gingerbread is said to have been an accident, possibly in
the early 1800s but, as usual, there is no contemporary documentation.

Lightness and hollowness have long been accepted features of the
gingerbread. These attributes may have come from early use of chemical
raising agents. Several formulae include bicarbonate of ammonia, used in
the first half of the nineteenth century before the development of modern
baking powders. George Mercer, a confectioner in the town in the early
nineteenth century, is said to have evolved the recipe. It passed through
several families and became famous as Caitlin's Grantham Gingerbreads.
Although Caitlin's recipe is not made commercially at present, the
gingerbread is still being produced in Southwell, Nottinghamshire.
Florence White (1932) notes a record of Grantham gingerbread being
sold as fairings. White gingerbreads, known also as Lincolnshire white
gingerbreads, and Norfolk fair buttons were similar confections.

Published recipes vary slightly; they call for equal quantities of flour and sugar; the proportion of butter is variable, but falls between one-third to two-thirds the weight of flour. They were mixed by either creaming or by rubbing in. Eggs are sometimes, but not always, added to make a soft dough; milk was an alternative. Volatile salts (ammonium bicarbonate) are the raising agent in most recipes. Commercial recipes state the dough should rest overnight before it is made into a rope then cut into slices to form the biscuits.

REGION OF PRODUCTION:

EAST MIDLANDS, GRANTHAM (LINCOLNSHIRE).

Bakewell Pudding

DESCRIPTION:

DIMENSIONS: A LARGE EXAMPLE IS AN OVAL 140MM BY 170MM, 50MM DEEP. WEIGHT: ABOUT 550G. FORM: A PUFF PASTRY CASE WITH A SMOOTH SEMI-TRANSPARENT FILLING WITH A THIN LAYER OF JAM BETWEEN THE PASTRY AND THE FILLING; THE PASTRY EXTENDS WELL ABOVE THE FILLING. COLOUR: THE PASTRY IS GOLDEN BROWN; THE FILLING IS BROWNED ON THE SURFACE BUT A DEEP YELLOW WHEN CUT. FLAVOUR: RICH, WITH EGGS AND ALMONDS.

HISTORY:

Bakewell pudding as it is now understood consists of a pastry case baked with a layer of jam (strawberry or raspberry) covered by a filling of eggs, sugar, butter and ground almonds. In Bakewell there is a story that the pudding originated as a result of a mistake by a cook at a local inn. This is almost certainly a legend. The earliest recipe, given by Eliza Acton (1845), is essentially an inch-thick, rich custard of egg yolks, butter, sugar and flavouring – ratafia (almond liqueur) is suggested – poured over a layer of mixed jams and candied citron or orange peel. There is no pastry lining. Miss Acton noted, 'This pudding is famous not only in Derbyshire, but in several of our

northern counties, where it is usually served on all holiday-occasions.'
In this form, it bears some resemblance to various cheesecake recipes
of the preceding century, or, in its omission of milk curds, the
'transparent' puddings popular in the same era (Grigson, 1984). Acton
drew parallels between her recipe and one 'known in the south' as
Alderman's pudding. Her preference was for the latter; Bakewell
pudding was not, in her opinion, 'very refined'. Mrs Beeton (1861)
gave a recipe much closer to the one we know. It included ground
almonds in the custard, omitted the candied peel, reduced the quantity
of jam and added a lining of puff pastry (or a layer of breadcrumbs
instead of paste for a plainer pudding). Since then, there has been a
tendency to less jam and more almonds.

PRODUCTION:
There are 3 producers in Bakewell but it is now manufactured
throughout the country. The Bakewell recipes are trade secrets.

REGION OF PRODUCTION:
NORTH MIDLANDS, BAKEWELL (DERBYSHIRE).

Lincolnshire Plum Bread

DESCRIPTION:
A BATCH LOAF OF LOW, ROUNDED SHAPE, 120MM LONG, 80MM WIDE,
35MM DEEP, WEIGHING ABOUT 300G. COLOUR: DEPENDS PARTLY ON THE
INGREDIENTS, ESPECIALLY THE TYPE OF SUGAR USED; GENERALLY A
DEEP GOLD OUTSIDE WITH THE DRIED FRUIT SHOWING PROMINENTLY;
THE CRUMB BEIGE, SPECKLED WITH FRUIT; SOME EXAMPLES ARE A
DEEPER BROWN. FLAVOUR AND TEXTURE: SWEET, LIGHTLY SPICED; THE
VERSIONS WHICH USE LARD AS SHORTENING HAVE CLOSER TEXTURE
AND CAN BE GREASY.

HISTORY:
Plum in this context refers to the dried fruit in the bread. This usage
was once common (e.g. plum pudding) suggesting the form has a long
history. No early references have yet been found in the area; the earliest

date which has been established is that of a recipe used by one of the bakers who make the bread, Derek Myers and Sons, which is some 100 years old. Although this is especially associated with Lincolnshire, it probably shares a common history with other spiced, sweetened and fruited breads. Plum bread is rich and heavy and distinguished by the use of lard as a shortening, reflecting the region's strong emphasis on pork products. It is often eaten with cheese. Although available all the year round, it is more popular at Christmas.

TECHNIQUE:

Ingredients include plain flour, lard, sultanas, currants, mixed peel, spices, sugar, eggs, yeast, salt and water. Recipes vary in detail, and the lard may be replaced with other fats. There is a short bulk fermentation, but final proof after shaping is up to 3 hours. It is baked for about 75 minutes at 160°C.

REGION OF PRODUCTION:
EAST MIDLANDS, LINCOLNSHIRE.

Melton Hunt Cake

DESCRIPTION:

A CAKE, 140MM DIAMETER, 40MM DEEP. WEIGHT: 1KG. COLOUR: DARK BROWN, FLECKED WITH DARK FRUIT, THE TOP DECORATED WITH ALMONDS AND GLACÉ CHERRIES IN CONCENTRIC CIRCLES; THE CUT SURFACES SHOW PLENTIFUL CURRANTS, RAISINS, FLAKED ALMONDS AND A FEW CHERRIES. FLAVOUR AND TEXTURE: RICH, WITH SLIGHT TOFFEE-CARAMEL NOTE, CLOSE TEXTURE.

HISTORY:

The Melton Hunt cake is in the tradition of the enriched, fruited and spiced cakes of earlier centuries. By the mid-nineteenth century the modern cake raised with beaten egg and baking powder had evolved and the Melton Hunt cake is of this type. The exact recipe was created in 1854 by John Dickinson. He started making it for the members of the Melton Hunt (the town has been famous as a centre for fox-hunting for over 200 years). It was originally intended to be eaten with the stirrup cup as the huntsmen assemble at the meet. The modern recipe has not changed and great effort is made to ensure the finest ingredients. It is the sole property of one company in Melton Mowbray.

REGION OF PRODUCTION:
MIDLANDS, MELTON MOWBRAY (LEICESTERSHIRE).

Marmite

DESCRIPTION:
MARMITE IS A STICKY, SHINY SUBSTANCE, SO DARK BROWN AS TO BE ALMOST BLACK. THE FLAVOUR IS SALTY, REMINISCENT OF BROWN FRIED ONIONS OR CONCENTRATED MEAT JUICES.

HISTORY:
Marmite is prepared from the yeast generated as a by-product of the brewing industry in Burton-upon-Trent. The Marmite Food Co. was formed in 1902 to exploit some of the nutritive qualities of yeast discovered during the nineteenth century. The original process, which had been developed on the Continent, was adjusted to yeast produced by British methods of fermentation. The discovery of vitamins boosted the popularity of Marmite. It was shown to be a good source of B vitamins. Output has grown steadily through the twentieth century. There is no other producer. Marmite is a registered trademark.

TECHNIQUE:
After the fresh yeast arrives at the factory, the main process it undergoes is autolysis: this takes place in large tanks. The yeast breaks down and releases its nutrients into solution. The fluid is centrifuged and filtered to remove the cell walls which are not required in the finished product. It is then condensed under vacuum until the correct consistency is reached. Finally, it is blended and flavoured with vegetable extracts and spices.

REGION OF PRODUCTION:
EAST MIDLANDS.

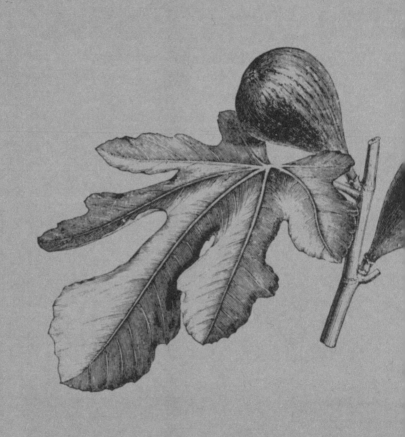

West Midlands

Asparagus (Evesham)

DESCRIPTION:

IN ENGLAND ASPARAGUS IS USUALLY CUT IN SPEARS ABOUT 20CM LONG, 10–15MM DIAMETER. IT IS SOLD IN BUNDLES OF 250G OR 500G. IT IS BRIGHT MID-GREEN, PURPLISH OR WHITE TOWARDS THE BASE.

HISTORY:

Gerard recognized in 1636 that asparagus grew wild; he identified several sites on the eastern side of the country. But it was the garden plant, heavily manured and intensively cultivated, that was especially valued. The Romans appreciated it too. Cato, in the first Roman agricultural handbook, gave instructions for creating an asparagus bed that were not so different from those broadcast today. He also drew the distinction between the wild and the garden plants. It continued as a serious delicacy on the Roman table; even Anthimus, the sixth-century Gothic ambassador to a Frankish king in the barbarian North, could discourse on its culinary and medicinal virtues. While the Anglo-Saxons made reference to it in their leechdoms or medical treatises, the plant appears to have dropped from the cook's provisions throughout the Middle Ages, only being reintroduced to British shores at the end of Henry VIII's reign.

It was still an unimproved oddity in England in 1614, the year Giacomo Castelvetro wrote his submission on vegetables and fruit to Lucy, Countess of Bedford (1989). 'When I see the weedy specimens of this noble plant for sale in London I never cease to wonder why no one has yet taken the trouble to improve its cultivation,' he wrote, happy that matters were better managed in his native Italy. London gardeners were soon to take up the cudgels. The playwright Philip Massinger mentions an asparagus garden in *The City Madam* (1632), and 30 years later Pepys goes to buy his spears from another. Soon the whole city was ringed by growers, especially in Mortlake and Deptford. As the market developed, so did the production of early, forced spears, grown on hotbeds to peak in January rather than from March to May (Thick, 1998).

By the eighteenth century, cultivation was general. Martha Bradley (1756) wrote, 'We are now advanced into the middle of March, a season at which he is but an indifferent gardener ... who has not good asparagus for the table.' Generally, the British seem to have preferred long, thin green spears, of more intense flavour than the fleshy, pale stems that were esteemed on the Continent.

Where London went, the rest of the country followed, and soon other districts had market gardens producing asparagus for local towns. The Vale of Evesham, running south-west from Stratford on Avon in Warwickshire to the River Severn, developed as an area producing early fruit and vegetables. Horticultural expansion was helped by the presence of the large manufacturing towns close by, and the early development of canal and railway transport through the region, linking it with wider markets in Bristol and London. Evesham and asparagus, particularly in the first decades of this century, became identified. More recently, the industry here has declined relative to that of Lincolnshire and East Anglia.

There is a second apparent regional connection in respect of this plant, Bath asparagus. In fact, it is a counterfeit asparagus, the wood star of Bethlehem (*Ornithogalum pyrenaicum*), that grows in the woods and waste around the cities of Bath and Bristol. 'Eaten by the common people,' was one dismissive remark, although in living memory it has been gathered in sufficient quantity to be sold in local markets. It resembles sprue, the very thin spears of true asparagus that are gathered from young plants or as a by-product of a healthy bed.

TECHNIQUE:

Local climatic conditions allow crops in the Vale of Evesham to ripen 10–14 days ahead of the main growing regions in the east of

Britain. Asparagus used to be a crop to utilize the ground between trees in plum orchards. The soils are heavy clay, and the long-established variety, still much used, is Connover's Colossal, although heavy cropping F1 hybrids are also now grown. After preparation of the ground into ridges, young plants are transplanted in peat nodules. The first picking takes place after 2–3 years, and the plants are left on site for up to 20 years. The shoots may be left entirely green, or partially earthed up and picked 'green-white', that is, with the lower parts blanched. In the past, asparagus was presented for market in bundles of 60 or 120 spears, bound with osier twigs tied in traditional patterns. This craft is now in decline, but can still be seen at the annual asparagus auction held at the Fleece Inn, Bretforton, in the latter part of May, when large bundles of very high quality asparagus are sold.

REGION OF PRODUCTION:
WEST MIDLANDS, THE VALE OF EVESHAM.

Black Currant

DESCRIPTION:
DEEP PURPLE-BLACK BERRIES ABOUT 1CM DIAMETER, STRIPPED FROM THE BRANCHES. FLAVOUR: SWEET, WITH DISTINCTIVE MUSKY AROMA. VERY RICH IN VITAMIN C.

HISTORY:
The black currant, *Ribes nigrum*, appears to have been introduced as a garden plant by John Tradescant in 1611. MacCarthy (1989) says they were taken to be the fruit from which currants (which are actually dried grapes) were produced, hence the name. Black currants were at first disliked because the leaves and berries have a strong smell; red and white currants were preferred (Roach, 1985). During the eighteenth century the fruit slowly gained acceptance, and was used in puddings, tarts and jellies, but its chief attraction has always been medicinal, as a base for drinks and potions. It was, indeed, only after it had been

discovered to contain abnormally high quantities of vitamin C that the black currant became a plant universally adopted by English gardeners.

The black currant is native to northern climates. It has never, therefore, figured in cuisines of Mediterranean countries, and is only grown in France (principally in Bordeaux and Burgundy) as a base for a cordial. Britain is its culinary stronghold and there are several historic cultivars, particularly Black Naples and Baldwin, that are important here.

Black currants have their longest history as a dessert crop in Herefordshire. According to Keith Worsley, as early as 1643 they were exported to London, packed in ice, carried by boat down the River Wye and thence round the coast. Commercial considerations to do with picking and productiveness have affected the production of black currants for processing, but Baldwin remains an outstanding variety, sought for its flavour, and still cultivated in Herefordshire for the dessert market.

Ninety per cent of black currants grown in Britain are used for processing, mostly to make cordial. It is said that a proportion of fruit from the variety Baldwin is essential to the flavour of 'Ribena', the best-known brand of black currant drink in Britain. Dessert black currants, of which Baldwin is the principal representative, are also used for summer pudding, pies, sauces, jams, jellies and to flavour fools and yoghurt. Black currant tea, made with jam and hot water, is a soothing drink for children with a cold; black currants are also made into pastilles.

TECHNIQUE:

Black currants are grown on bushes out of doors. Soil type is not of primary importance, but water supply is. Herefordshire, an area in which these are an accepted crop, is bounded to the west by the Black Mountains and the Brecon Beacons, high ground which creates a rain shadow area. Just enough rain spills across from these hills to give the right conditions for successful black currant cultivation. The climate is also relatively frost-free, but cold enough to provide the necessary vernalization required for British cultivars of black currants. Fruit for the dessert market is usually harvested by hand from bushes in their first year of growth; mechanical harvesting can be used for older bushes. Replanting takes place every 12–15 years. Baldwin is relatively low yielding, and the cultivation of it and other old varieties is diminishing. New cultivars such as Ben Alder, Ben Tiron and Ben Lomond developed at the Scottish Crop Research Institute yield almost three times as much, with increased disease resistance, but are not considered to have such a fine flavour. As harvesting by hand is labour intensive, the pick-your-own market is increasingly important.

REGION OF PRODUCTION:
WEST MIDLANDS.

Black Worcester Pear

DESCRIPTION:

A COOKING PEAR; LARGE AND ROUNDED; DARK MAHOGANY SKIN WITH RUSSET FRECKLES; SMALL AREAS OF ROUGH SKIN; SHARP, BITTER AND HARD WHEN RAW, SOFTENS ON COOKING.

HISTORY:

Although the wild pear is found growing in Britain, it is doubted that it is indigenous. In any event, its fruit is hardly palatable and we benefited from centuries of breeding by the Greeks and Romans, then the French and Belgians (above all other nations) to create the range of fruit we have grown with enthusiasm from the Middle Ages (more specifically, from the Norman Conquest) until today.

The pear does not grow true from seed. It is best grafted. However, seedlings often arise and give us new cultivars. The pear, like the apple, is a species of infinite variety. Like the apple, again, there is a broad distinction between those suitable for eating and those for cooking alone. Cooking pears were termed wardens or wardons in later medieval England, taking their name from the abbey of Wardon in

Bedfordshire – no one knows the reason why. There was also a third category of pear, not really recognized until the sixteenth century, which was suitable for making perry.

All these pears proliferated as a multitude of varieties – comparable to the multiplication of apples and plums. Often the breeds were local, sometimes not spreading beyond the village or valley of their discovery. John Gerard expressed this nicely in 1597 when he denied himself the pleasure of listing all the varieties 'as it would fill a whole volume, each county having its own'. John Parkinson mentioned 'the Norwich, the Worcester, the Warwicke, the Arundel and the Petworth' in his *Paradisi in Sole* of 1629.

The Worcester was a warden or baking pear. The West Midlands region had begun to take its pears seriously with the development of perry, the cider made from pears. Many early references to perry have been gathered by Davies (1993): they emphasize its strong links with the county of Worcester, especially in Tudor and Stuart times. One writer noted it as a product of Kent, Sussex and Worcestershire; another made a distinction – perhaps reflecting commonly accepted reality – cider in Kent but perry in Worcestershire. Perry was at first, it seems, made from wild hedgerow pears, but as production increased, so did the requirement for raw material.

A preoccupation with pears, therefore, may be the reason for Queen Elizabeth I permitting the inclusion of 'three pears sable' in the coat of arms of the city of Worcester when she visited in 1575. The heraldry may also be the explanation why the Worcester is now the Black Worcester. What is certain is that this variety has been recorded, and linked to the city, for many centuries.

The tree grows very tall, and was planted in hedgerows or in orchards as a windbreak tree: 'Worcestershire is a pleasant, fruitful, and rich county abounding in corn, woods, pastures, hills, and valleys, every hedge and highway beset with fruit, but especially with pears, where-of they make a pleasant drink called perry which they sell for a penny a quart, though better than ever you tasted in London,' wrote the

Roundhead Nehemiah Wharton during the Civil War (Davies, 1993). More lyrically, the poet John Phillips carolled,

> '...the sturdy pear-tree here
> Will rise luxuriant, and with toughest root
> Pierce the obstructing grit, and restive marle.
> Thus nought is useless made...'

The Black Worcester is disease resistant, and the fruit keeps without being given any special attention for several months. Today, interest is as much for the emblematic significance and the genetic material it holds as stomachic delight. A scheme to encourage the planting of the Black Worcester Pear, together with other local apple and pear cultivars, is being run by the County Council in conjunction with the local agricultural college.

TECHNIQUE:
No particular method of cultivation is attached to this tree; at present it survives as a curiosity, growing untended in hedges and parks.

REGION OF PRODUCTION:
WEST MIDLANDS, WORCESTERSHIRE.

Pershore Plum

DESCRIPTION:
A MEDIUM TO LARGE PLUM, OVAL IN SHAPE AND YELLOW IN COLOUR; A CULINARY PLUM, THE FLAVOUR OF THE RAW FRUIT IS NOT PARTICULARLY GOOD.

HISTORY:
This plum was discovered by George Crooke growing as a seedling in Tiddesley Woods near the town of Pershore in 1827 (Smith, 1978). It is part of a similar sequence of events as noticed already under the Cambridge Gage (p. 3) – a chance seedling, thereafter propagated by sucker and extremely popular in the district of its discovery. In the

Pershore example, the timing was also fortunate. By the 1840s, Worcestershire (in which Pershore and most of the Vale of Evesham lie) was important for supplying plums to the markets in the Midland towns immediately to the north (Roach, 1985). A combination of other factors, including the expansion of market gardening on smallholdings, led to an increase in plum growing; the availability of a local variety, easily propagated from suckers, encouraged this. There was also greater demand for plums for processing, especially jam manufacture and canning, for which Pershore is a suitable variety.

This variety also had a substantial effect on British plum cultivation in general, as it provided strong rootstock for grafting, and has been important in the development of new cultivars. This plum is also called the Yellow Egg – for its colour – and there is a Purple Pershore, too, which has the same season and is also useful in canning and jam making. The Purple is a cross of Early Rivers and Diamond made by a local grower in the 1870s.

TECHNIQUE:

The Vale of Evesham runs south-west towards the river Severn. It has a slightly milder climate than the surrounding area, and has long been known for the production of fruit and vegetables, especially early asparagus and plums. Provided the soil is correct and the land sheltered from frost, plums do well. A band of clay outcropping along the Vale sides is well-suited to plum cultivation: it holds moisture well and escapes the frosts to which the valley floor is susceptible. Most of the orchards are located where the ground begins to rise at the edges and occupy poorer soils than other crops grown locally (such as salads). Old orchards are on strong rootstocks, giving large trees. Pershore Yellow Egg can be propagated from suckers. After the first 2 years, little maintenance beyond light pruning is carried out.

REGION OF PRODUCTION:

WEST MIDLANDS, PERSHORE (WORCESTERSHIRE).

Worcester Pearmain Apple

DESCRIPTION:

AN EARLY DESSERT APPLE. DESCRIBED BY MORGAN & RICHARDS (1993) AS A MEDIUM-SIZED APPLE (5–7CM DIAMETER), OF ROUND-CONICAL SHAPE, SOMETIMES SLIGHTLY LOPSIDED, AND SLIGHTLY RIBBED; THE BASIN IS NARROW, OF MEDIUM DEPTH TO SHALLOW, AND SLIGHTLY RIBBED, OFTEN WITH FIVE BEADS; THE EYE SMALL AND CLOSED, THE SEPALS SMALL AND QUITE DOWNY, THE CAVITY OF MEDIUM WIDTH AND DEPTH, AND RUSSET LINED; THE STALK IS SMALL AND QUITE THICK; THE COLOUR OF THE SKIN IS CHARACTERIZED BY A BRIGHT RED FLUSH WITH SOME FAINT RED STRIPES ON A ON A GREENISH YELLOW OR PALE YELLOW BACKGROUND, WITH LENTICELS QUITE CONSPICUOUS AS RUSSET DOTS; THE FLESH IS WHITE. THE FLAVOUR IS VERY SWEET, WITH AN INTENSE STRAWBERRY NOTE AND FIRM JUICY FLESH.

HISTORY:

The word pearmain to denote apple varieties has been in use in English since the late twelfth century. Early pearmains were primarily for cider. Both Winter and Summer Pearmains were known. A variety known as Old Pearmain is in the collection at Brogdale, but it is not certain if this is the true medieval pearmain.

The Worcester Pearmain is a relative newcomer, having arisen in the 1870s. It was commercialized shortly afterwards, and has been important ever since. It is believed to have been a seedling of a much older variety, the Devonshire Quarrenden, first mentioned in the late seventeenth century. The strawberry flavour seems characteristic of several early dessert apples, including Ben's Red, also sometimes known as Quarrenden, and the true Devonshire Quarrenden.

Several other varieties fall into the category of early dessert apples, including Discovery, raised just after the Second World War. This, too, has a detectable element of strawberry in its flavour. It claims the Worcester Pearmain as a parent but has eclipsed it commercially. The other apple which probably played a role in the ancestry of Discovery, the Beauty of Bath, is no longer grown commercially. Tydeman's Early, another apple with the Worcester in its ancestry, also has a strawberry flavour. Other early dessert apples which are still available are Epicure (Bedfordshire), Norfolk Royal (Norfolk), and James Grieve (raised in Scotland, but now widely grown commercially in Europe).

Worcester Pearmain is high in tannin and can be used effectively to produce a cider in the style of the West Country. It is also used as a pollinator for Bramley's Seedling.

TECHNIQUE:

See Bramley's Seedling (East Anglia) for more information about rootstocks. Optimum pollination time for Worcester Pearmain is early to mid-May; the tree is of medium vigour and is a heavy cropper, and produces fruit buds partially at the tips of new growth. Picking is by hand in early to mid-September. Grading is by diameter (sizes are set according to variety) and by quality into Grade 1 or Grade 2. Early dessert apples are not expected to keep for long; Worcester Pearmain is no exception, and is only available for about 6 weeks.

REGION OF PRODUCTION:

WEST MIDLANDS; SOUTH ENGLAND.

Hereford Hops Cheese

DESCRIPTION:

PRESSED, UNPASTEURIZED COW'S MILK CHEESE WITH COATING OF HOPS, IN 3 SIZES: 7CM DIAMETER, 7CM HIGH; 12CM DIAMETER, 8CM HIGH; 16CM DIAMETER, 4CM HIGH. WEIGHT: APPROXIMATELY 400G, 1.2KG, AND 2KG. COLOUR: PALE SMOOTH CURD WITH COATING OF DRIED HOPS. FLAVOUR: RICH, CREAMY, DELICATE LEMON TASTE, CONTRASTING WITH SAVOURY HOP FLAVOUR.

HISTORY:

The Hereford area has no great tradition of cheese-making, save probably on a small scale by farmers' wives (Rance, 1982). However, in this century various people have experimented with the craft, including Ellen Yeld who evolved 'Little Hereford', for small dairies, shortly before 1920. Oral tradition collected by Nicholas Hogetts, the maker of Hereford Hops, states that local farmers used once to have a habit of placing cheeses in barrels of hops to preserve them, and that local tastes in cheese varied, tending towards a higher cream content in the west of the area. Hereford Hops cheese evolved from these traditions, making use of local ingredients (hops) and skills. The name 'Hereford Hops' is protected.

TECHNIQUE:

Unpasteurized milk from a designated herd of British Friesian cattle is used. A small quantity of starter is added, followed by vegetarian rennet. The curd is cut into cubes of about 1cm and left to settle for 20 minutes. It is scalded at 32.5°C, after which the cheese is drained, the curd broken by hand, salted (2 per cent) and filled into hoops. It is pressed for 2 days under gradually increasing pressure. On removal from the hoops, the cheese is allowed to dry for about 5 days then coated with hops and matured a further 10 weeks.

REGION OF PRODUCTION:

WEST MIDLANDS, HEREFORD AND WORCESTERSHIRE.

Fidget Pie

DESCRIPTION:

A COOKED PORK, HAM OR BACON, VEGETABLE AND APPLE RAISED PIE; ABOUT 18CM DIAMETER, 5.5CM DEEP, WEIGHING 1500G. DEEP GOLD PASTRY CASE WITH CRIMPED EDGES; FILLINGS VARY A LITTLE, BUT ARE USUALLY COMPOSED OF LAYERS OF PINK HAM, GAMMON OR CURED PORK, WITH PALER LAYERS OF POTATO, APPLE AND ONION. THE FLAVOUR OF THE HAM OR PORK PREDOMINATES, WITH APPLE AND VEGETABLES AS A BLAND, SWEET COUNTER-BALANCE. SEASONING SOMETIMES INCLUDES SAGE.

HISTORY:

Fidget (or fitchett) pie has a persistent association with harvest time and was made in much of the Midlands, though apparently especially popular in Shropshire.

Early pork pies, for instance Nott (1726), included apples with the meat. Regional affiliation for the combination is proposed by Hannah Glasse (1747) who gives 2 recipes for Cheshire pork pies. One is a raised pie with fresh pork, pippins (sweet apples) and white wine; the other, 'for the sea', consists of fat, salt pork and potatoes. Joseph Wright (1896–1905) records that fitchett pie, in Cheshire, was a pie given to the reapers at harvest home, and was composed of apples, onions and bacon fat in equal quantities. Apparently cheese was sometimes substituted for the bacon in the West Midlands, but this was a departure from the old usage. The pie was reputed to smell foully during baking (perhaps it was thought to smell like a polecat; 'fitchett' was a dialect name for these animals). However, Lizzie Boyd (1988) suggests that the name comes from the term 'fitched', meaning five-sided, referring to the original shape of the pie.

Recipes for fidget pie appear in many books on English country cooking published during the twentieth century. Hartley (1954) states that the area around Market Harborough made especially good ones; White (1932) describes one from Shropshire; and a recipe from Huntingdon appears in a collection issued by the magazine *Farmer's Weekly* in 1963.

The mixture of meat and apples – mutton, pork or beef, in this case – is also found in another regional dish, Devonshire squab pie. This is identified as a speciality late in the seventeenth century, although it is no longer commercially produced. Bradley (1756) wrote of it: 'This is a particular dish, some are very fond of it; a right Devonshireman will prefer it to the best and nicest of all ...'

TECHNIQUE:

A filling of pork, fresh or cured, and apples is essential; onions, potatoes, stock, wine and seasoning are usual. The pie could be made in a dish topped with pastry and eaten hot; or it could be a raised pie produced for carrying away and eating hot or cold. The former was made for domestic consumption only; the latter is sometimes seen on sale. The meat is diced, and apples and vegetables prepared. They are placed in the crust in layers. Seasoning, wine or stock is added. The pie is covered with a pastry top, the edges crimped, the centre decorated and glazed with egg. It is baked at 160–170°C for up to 90 minutes.

REGION OF PRODUCTION:
MIDLANDS.

Old Horned Hereford Cattle

DESCRIPTION:
THE DRESSED WEIGHT FOR A CARCASS FROM A 20-MONTH STEER IS ABOUT 275KG. OLD HORNED HEREFORDS HAVE SHORT LEGS, HEAVY DEWLAPS AND DEEP BODIES. THOSE WITH IMPORTED BLOOD ARE TALLER AND LONGER-BODIED. THE MEAT IS VERY WELL MARBLED, WITH DEPTH OF FLAVOUR AND VERY TENDER.

HISTORY:
The Old Horned Hereford, now designated a rare breed, represents the genetic line from which the millions of Hereford cattle found in the New World originally sprang. According to Peter Symonds, a breeder, the origins of all Herefords go back to the late eighteenth and early nineteenth centuries. At this time, various breeders in the Herefordshire area, which lies on the Welsh Marches and was, at that time, relatively isolated, began to improve local cattle. Benjamin Tompkins (1745–1815) did much to lay the foundations. In the 1840s, John Hewer, deciding that it would benefit the stock to have distinctive markings, deliberately bred Hereford cattle to have a white face and a red-brown body, the pattern which persists today. At the same period, a stud book was started. All Hereford cattle were once horned (the polled variety was developed through interbreeding with the naturally polled Galloway or with North American stock). In the late nineteenth century, Hereford bulls were much exported to the New World to upgrade the existing cattle. During the 1950s, restrictions on the importing of breeding cattle into Britain were relaxed and Horned Hereford bulls from North America were used to

give extra height to the domestic strain. The vast majority of Hereford cattle now in Britain are of mixed British-North American blood: these are defined as Horned Hereford and Polled Hereford. Recently, an initiative by the Rare Breeds Survival Trust to protect genetic material in the original English Hereford has resulted in the naming of the indigenous, uncrossed cattle as Old Horned Hereford to distinguish them from the modern variants.

TECHNIQUE:

The agriculture of Herefordshire and environs is traditionally mixed, with some arable land, apple and pear orchards and good pasture, plus rougher grazing on higher ground. Hereford cattle were originally three-purpose, used for draught oxen (this continued up until 1939 on one estate), for milking, and for beef. The latter has been latterly the most important. In common with all British breeds, the cattle are hardy and flourish on grass alone; 'kings in grass castles' was one description of them earlier this century. The majority of breeders keep their cattle outdoors, except in late winter when they may be housed to prevent the pastures being damaged by the heavy animals trampling wet grassland. Supplementary feeding may be given to the breeding cows, in the form of hay or silage according to the individual farmer; some feed grain, although it is regarded as a virtue of the breed that this is unnecessary. Calves are born in spring or autumn, and remain with their mothers until naturally weaned. They are killed for beef at about 18–20 months.

One butcher, Andrew Sebire, runs an initiative to provide beef from Hereford cattle which is reared, slaughtered and butchered to tight specifications, and hung in the traditional way for 3–6 weeks. A large number of the modern breed reach the market, and the breed is also used commercially for crossing. There is one major herd of Old Horned Herefords in the native area and a handful of pedigree Horned or Polled herds. There are a couple of other large herds of Old Horned Herefords in the country at large, and several breeders with a few pedigree animals.

Scratchings

DESCRIPTION:

SALTED, CRISP, COOKED PIG SKIN; INDIVIDUAL PIECES MEASURE 2–10CM
LONG, 1–2CM WIDE. SOLD LOOSE OR IN BAGS OF 100G. COLOUR: DEEP
GOLD, POWDERY. FLAVOUR: SALTY, CRISP, SOMETIMES TOUGH.

HISTORY:

Originally the word referred to the crisp, cooked membrane left after
pig fat had been rendered. As scratchings are an inevitable by-product
of lard-making, they must have been available for centuries, but they
are little mentioned before the 1800s. Presumably, they were
considered inconsequential. It cannot be said that anyone set out with
the intention of making scratchings; they were there for whoever cared
to eat them at pig-killing time.

Wright (1896–1905) gives instances of the word from an area
stretching through the whole of middle England as far south as
Devon. This is still the broad region in which they are most found.
They were sometimes baked into a cake – mixed with flour – or they
were spread and eaten on bread. In the country round Birmingham,
the word could mean a specific dish of diced, fried leaf-lard eaten with
pepper and salt. The word has been extended to cover pieces of
crackling (crisply cooked pig skin), and the old types of scratchings are
now uncommon.

Scratchings are salted and sealed in plastic bags for sale as a snack;
they are widely available in pubs in the West Midlands and South
West England where they are a popular and thirst-provoking
accompaniment to beer.

TECHNIQUE:

The method for rendering lard involved cutting the fat small or
mincing it, soaking and then melting it over very low heat. The residue

of cooked connective tissue left after the fat had been poured off was the scratchings. Modern, factory-produced scratchings are made from pig skin with its underlying fat, baked until crisp.

REGION OF PRODUCTION:
MIDLANDS.

Tamworth Pig

DESCRIPTION:

A DRESSED CARCASS DESTINED FOR BACON WEIGHS AT LEAST 64KG. THEY MAY ALSO BE USED FOR FRESH PORK. THEY HAVE GOOD BACON CONFORMATION: LONG IN THE SIDES, LIGHT SHOULDERS AND WELL-FILLED HAMS. THEIR SANDY-RED BRISTLES DO NOT AFFECT THE SKIN, WHICH DRESSES WHITE. THE COLOUR OF THE MEAT DEPENDS TO AN EXTENT ON AGE AND FEEDING; IT IS SUCCULENT, WELL-FLAVOURED AND FINE-GRAINED.

HISTORY:

The Tamworth is sometimes known as the original English pig and is thought a descendant of the feral woodland pig. It is believed it was not cross-bred with animals of Chinese origin – a ploy much favoured for improving pigs in the early nineteenth century.

It has long been famous beyond the boundaries of Staffordshire and was the traditional British bacon pig, producing carcasses with long sides and fine hams. In the 1800s it was used for crossing with the Berkshire to produce bacon pigs (Samuel, 1860). Tamworths began to decline in popularity when, like many other old breeds, they were supplanted by leaner animals which matured in less time.

TECHNIQUE:

The Tamworth is exceptionally hardy, surviving on a minimal diet, foraging on grass and rough ground. It may be used to clear old pasture or scrub, can tolerate extremes of temperature and does not suffer from sunburn. Outdoor sows are generally kept in hard conditions except at farrowing, or if conditions are very muddy. They do not require special

It's a bit of a mystery what has happened to British food in the last century and how it lost its way… There was the move from rural areas to cities, the Second World War, the frozen Chicken Kiev school of thought, but none of them fairly can be blamed for a nation which likes its meat anonymous, pink and in plastic. Especially if, as a nation, we enjoy the rigours of British seasons, which will write a glorious menu for you.

To start the year, native oysters are in season, then sea kale, St George's mushrooms, gulls eggs, English asparagus, jersey royals and spring lamb. The summer brings strawberries and raspberries – my favourite season is around June, when broad beans are small, Berkswell Cheese is in fantastic condition, there are suckling kids around and I've got about a month and a half to fantasize about my first grouse. Before you know it, it's 12 August and delicious birds are falling from the sky – grouse, grey-legged partridge, pheasants and woodcock – and root vegetables are ready for harvesting. Undeniable goodness. How we've ignored this is a rum old do.

Fergus Henderson

FOUNDER, ST. JOHN RESTAURANT, LONDON

feeding, although many get supplementary dry rations and vegetable scraps. Tamworths are well suited to the present movement towards extensive agriculture. They can yield a lean carcass if required, although breeders prefer a degree of fat. In recent years a renewed interest in the breed has inspired work on the improvement of litter sizes, the number of pigs reared and their weaning weight.

The animals destined for bacon are killed at 8–9 months. After slaughter, the carcasses are dressed to yield sides suitable for bacon; there are regional and personal preferences in the exact shape of these. Until the mid-nineteenth century, a dry-salt cure was always used for bacon. It persists in some places, but modern light-brine cures work well with Tamworths, as their meat has an excellent flavour.

REGION OF PRODUCTION:
WEST MIDLANDS.

Banbury Cake

DESCRIPTION:

A POINTED OVAL SHAPE OF PASTRY WRAPPING A FRUIT FILLING; THE COLOUR IS PALE, WITH A CRISP, BUBBLED SUGAR COATING. DIMENSIONS: 150MM LONG, 60MM WIDE, 10–20MM DEEP. WEIGHT: 50–75G. FLAVOUR: RICH, DRIED FRUIT AND SPICES.

HISTORY:

In Ben Jonson's play *Bartholomew Fair* (1614) there is a character, Zeal-of-the-Land Busy, a Banbury baker whose cakes 'were served to bridals, may-poles, morrises and such profane feasts and meetings'. As Addison said in *the Tatler*, 'Banbury is a town known for cakes and zeal.' The first known recipe is given by Markham (1615), although the apparent form has changed over the years. A recipe book in 1655 contains complicated instructions headed, 'The Countess of Rutland's Receipt of making the rare Banbury Cake, which was so much admired at her Daughters (the Right Honourable the Lady Chaworths) Wedding.' It described a rich, sweet, spiced, yeast-

leavened dough divided into 2 portions. One was left plain, the other mixed with currants. That with currants was sandwiched between thin layers of the plain paste. Size was left to the cook's discretion, but if the quantities given were used for one cake, it would have weighed about 4kg. Similar cakes were known elsewhere, one example being the Shrewsbury Simnel. Another was the now extinct Coventry Godcake which was triangular. A third is the black bun, made in Scotland at New Year; Eccles and Chorley cakes are yet other relation. By the 1800s, Banbury cakes had become as small as we know them today. Dr Kitchiner (1822) cites a filling like that known in the seventeenth century but enclosed in puff pastry.

A shop in Parsons Street, already known in 1833 as 'The Original Cake Shop', was said to have been started by one Betty White in 1638. Subsequent owners are documented through the 1800s and Banbury cakes were exported in considerable numbers to India. They were also found in refreshment rooms on stations up and down the Great Western Railway, which ran through the town (Grigson, 1984).

An earlier method of packaging the cakes was preserved as an exhibit in the shop: a spherical basket with a domed lid on a rope handle. Baking ceased at the shop and attached tea-room in 1969 and the building was partially demolished. Recipes still in use in the town exhibit many variations, for example using cake crumbs in the middle layer of currants. Recently, supermarkets have started to sell items called Banbury cakes, but they make them square or round, not in the usual shape.

TECHNIQUE:

Puff pastry is cut into rounds. A filling of currants, candied peel, flour, butter, brown sugar, rose water, lemon essence, rum essence and nutmeg is sandwiched between the puff pastry. The edges are folded over to form a little roll. Then the cake is rolled out to elongate it, and given final shape by pressing to flatten, with the seam underneath. The tops are brushed with egg white and sprinkled with a pulverized sugar. They are baked for 20 minutes at 220°C.

Market Drayton Gingerbread

DESCRIPTION:

OBLONG FINGERS WITH LENGTHWISE RIDGES; SOLD IN BLOCKS OF 7, EACH 80MM LONG, 12MM WIDE, 10MM DEEP. WEIGHT: EACH FINGER APPROXIMATELY 20G. COLOUR: MID-BROWN. FLAVOUR AND TEXTURE: SWEET, SPICY WITH GINGER AND LEMON; HARD, WITH SHORT, CRISP TEXTURE.

HISTORY:

In the early 1800s, a baker named Thomas sold gingerbread similar to that made today in this small Shropshire town. A chain of named people have held the formula since Mr Thomas. By 1900 there were 4 gingerbread bakers and a flourishing postal export trade to the colonies. Billington, the family name now associated with the speciality, held the recipe for about 100 years to 1939–45. Wartime rationing limited the quantities which could be made; afterwards, it remained a little-known curiosity until the 1980s when it was revived.

A domestic recipe is given in a manuscript from the 1850s. The commercial recipes (of which there appear to have been at least 4 in existence at the time of its heyday) are kept secret. The characteristic ridged shape has been linked with the gingerbread as long as the Billingtons were involved in its manufacture. A hand-cranked machine for extruding ribbons of dough through a star-shaped nozzle – which imparts the ribs – was made for the firm and is still in use.

TECHNIQUE:

The ingredients are given as wheat flour, sugar, margarine, Golden Syrup, eggs, ground ginger, rum, spices, sodium bicarbonate and cream of tartar. The exact recipe and method are a trade secret. Ginger from both Cochin and Jamaica are quoted in connection with the recipe.

Pikelet

DESCRIPTION:

A CIRCULAR FLAT BREAD, WITH A PATTERN OF SMALL HOLES COVERING THE UPPER SURFACE, EDGES THINNER THAN THE CENTRE, AND A SLIGHTLY IRREGULAR SHAPE; 90–110MM DIAMETER, ABOUT 5MM DEEP. WEIGHT: ABOUT 30–35G. COLOUR: VERY PALE, ALMOST WHITE, WITH A LITTLE BROWN SPECKLING ON TOP; SMOOTH BROWN SURFACE UNDERNEATH. FLAVOUR AND TEXTURE: MILDLY SWEET, SPONGY; ALWAYS EATEN TOASTED.

A WELSH PIKELET, BOUGHT IN SWANSEA MARKET, IS THE SAME DIAMETER BUT THICKER (10–15MM) AND HEAVIER (75G).

HISTORY:

The word belongs to the dialects of the English Midlands, and indicates a small, rather thick, yeast-leavened griddle-bread, characterized by a spongy, holey surface. They are like crumpets, which are better known and usually thought a thicker, more regular bread baked in ring-shaped moulds. In some regions there is much confusion between the terms, not helped by the fact that the size of crumpets was more variable in the past. They ranged from 'large brownish dinner-plate size made with an admixture of brown flour ... to small, rather thick, very holey [ones] made in the Midlands' (Hartley, 1954).

The origin of the words pikelet and crumpet is problematic and derivations from Welsh are postulated. Joseph Wright (1896–1905) offers bara picklet, obsolete Welsh for yeast-leavened cakes of fine wheat flour, and crumpet may have derived from crempog, which meant a pancake or fritter (David, 1977). The proposed derivation of the Scottish crumpet should, however, be noted. The first known recipe for pikelet and crumpet-type products is 'tea crumpets' given by

Mrs Raffald (1769). These were made from a thick batter with milk and water, flour, yeast and eggs, which was cooked on a bakestone; the baker was instructed to 'let it run to the size of a tea saucer' and, 'when you want to use them roast them very crisp, and butter them'. The recipe suggests she is describing something which would now be regarded by most people as a pikelet.

While it is possible that both products have a common region of origin, the pikelet has remained a Northern and Welsh speciality, while the crumpet is universal through Britain. The chief difference is that pikelets may be irregular in shape if the batter is not contained on the bakestone by hoops or rings (as were invariably used for crumpets). However, many earlier writers claimed simply that pikelet was the Northern name for crumpet. The holes in the tops of both breads were caused by the batter being liquid enough to allow the yeast fermentation (sometimes reinforced by chemicals) to manifest itself. A griddle-cooked scone, which was not fermented, was smooth on both sides; a muffin, which was fermented but made with a stiffer dough, was also smooth, the fermentation acting upon the texture of the crumb, not forcing its way to the outside.

TECHNIQUE:

The flour used for pikelets and crumpets is usually softer than that used for the more bread-like muffin. Bicarbonate of soda is sometimes added to help the characteristic holey appearance on the top surface. A yeast-leavened batter of flour and water with a little sugar and cream of tartar is left to work for 45 minutes; extra water plus a little salt and bicarbonate of soda are added. The batter is deposited in small pools on a hot-plate, and the network of holes allowed to set. The industrial method is a scaled-up version of this process.

REGION OF PRODUCTION:

MIDLANDS; NORTH ENGLAND; SOUTH WALES.

Shrewsbury Cake

DESCRIPTION:

A ROUND BISCUIT WITH FLUTED EDGE, 70–80MM DIAMETER, 8MM
THICK. WEIGHT: ABOUT 30G. COLOUR: PALE GOLD, SPECKLED WITH
CURRANTS. FLAVOUR AND TEXTURE: SWEET, WITH SLIGHT LEMON
PERFUME, CRISP.

HISTORY:

Doubt surrounds the first mentions of these cakes, also called biscuits
(Lloyd, 1931). Cakes are often mentioned in the bailiffs' accounts for
the town during the 1500s and in contemporary correspondence.
Their ingredients may be unknown, but they were already famous for
their crisp, brittle texture. Lord Herbert of Cherbury sent his guardian
in 1602, 'a kind of cake which our countrey people use and made in no
place in England but in Shrewsbury... Measure not my love by
substance of it, which is brittle, but by the form of it which is circular.'

Just this brittleness was celebrated by the playwright Congreve in
The Way of The World (1700) when he used the expression 'as short as
a Shrewsbury cake'. The earliest recipe, in Eliza Smith (1728), is for a
sweet biscuit spiced with cinnamon and nutmeg. A hundred years later
the Reverend Hugh Oven noted that Shrewsbury had always been
distinguished for 'a kind of sweet, flat cake' and that great quantities
were sold in the town. A reference to them in *The Ingoldsby Legends*
(1840) ensured their fame, for the poem mentions a maker of
Shrewsbury cakes named Pailin. Whether he was a historical figure
has never been quite established. It is possible that a Miss Hill,
daughter of one of the town's confectioners, married a Mr Palin, but
no satisfactory link with Shrewsbury cakes has been demonstrated.
Inspired by the poem, the trademark 'Pailin's Original Shrewsbury
Cakes' originated in the late nineteenth century. They were made to a
secret recipe by Phillip's Stores Ltd until the outbreak of the Second
World War. During the war and the years of rationing which followed,
the firm gave it all up because of shortage of ingredients, especially
butter. Today, though Shrewsbury cakes are known, little curiosity

about them is expressed by the inhabitants themselves. An enquiry to a local bakery producing 'Shrewsbury Biscuits' yielded only a few uninterested comments and it seems this once famous speciality has lost its identity and is ripe for a revival.

TECHNIQUE:

The present whereabouts of the recipe used by Phillip's is unknown, but many others are extant. They are for a shortbread. Simon (1960) mixes equal parts of flour, butter and sugar into a paste with one egg white per 250g of mixture. This is baked at about 160°C for 20 minutes. Earlier instructions, such as Hannah Glasse (1747), have twice as much flour which makes something crisper. Rose water is often mentioned as a flavouring, as well as spices such as cinnamon, nutmeg and caraway.

REGION OF PRODUCTION:

WEST MIDLANDS, SHREWSBURY (SHROPSHIRE).

Simnel Cake

DESCRIPTION:

A ROUND CAKE WITH A HORIZONTAL LAYER OF ALMOND PASTE THROUGH THE MIDDLE, AND ANOTHER ON TOP WITH A CHARACTERISTIC DECORATION OF 11 BALLS OF ALMOND PASTE; SOMETIMES THIS IS REPLACED BY SUGAR ICING WITH DECORATIONS CONSIDERED SUITABLE FOR THE SEASON. IT MEASURES 160–300MM ACROSS, ABOUT 80MM HIGH. COLOUR: REDDISH, GOLDEN-BROWN OR CREAMY-YELLOW CRUMB, SPECKLED WITH DRIED FRUIT. FLAVOUR: SWEET, RICH, WITH ALMONDS AND DRIED FRUIT.

HISTORY:

The cake was originally associated with Mid-Lent Sunday, a time when the Lenten fast was relaxed to allow consumption of richer foods, adding variety to an otherwise monotonous diet. This day was also known as Mothering Sunday: pilgrimages were made to the mother cathedral of a diocese. Later, the holiday developed into the secular festival of Mother's Day. During the nineteenth century it was said that servant girls were allowed to bake simnel cakes to take as presents for their mothers when they visited their families.

The development of the simnel cake had 3 overlapping phases (Wilson, 1985). In its early medieval form, simnel was classified as a type of bread, made from fine white flour (the word is derived from Latin *simila*, the whitest, most finely ground flour). It may have been lightly enriched, and was said to have been 'twice baked'. By the seventeenth century, the recipes had been greatly enriched with dried fruit (especially currants), almonds and spices, including saffron. The dough was enclosed in a pastry crust and the whole was boiled before being painted with egg yolk and baked, giving a very hard exterior. This form, illustrated in a fifteenth-century dictionary, survived into the mid-nineteenth century as the Shrewsbury simnel. Several other localities made simnels to their own specification. The Bury simnel, from Lancashire, was one of the better known and was sent by post all over the country, a trade only stopped by the imposition of rationing during the Second World War. This was a yeast-leavened fruit cake containing high proportions of dried fruit

and ground almonds. The pastry crust disappeared from most simnel recipes during the late nineteenth century and they evolved into their present form, related to the rich fruit cakes characteristic of English cookery. The almond paste layers and decoration are of twentieth-century origin, replacing an earlier tradition of preserved fruits and sugar flowers. In its present form, the cake is eaten at Easter, and the 11 balls of almond paste are said to represent the 11 loyal disciples. Its connection with Mothering Sunday is defunct and the apparent regional affiliations mentioned above have been severed.

TECHNIQUE:

Many small bakeries make simnel cakes using craft methods. Two types are recognized: yeast-leavened, and a conventional rich fruit cake.

REGION OF PRODUCTION:

WEST MIDLANDS; NORTH WEST ENGLAND.

Staffordshire Oatcake

DESCRIPTION:

CIRCULAR FLATBREAD, SIMILAR TO A THICK PANCAKE; ABOUT 200MM
DIAMETER, 4MM THICK. WEIGHT: ABOUT 110G. COLOUR: PALE BROWN,
SPECKLED, SMOOTH ON UNDERSIDE AND FULL OF SMALL HOLES ON TOP.
FLAVOUR AND TEXTURE: OATY, SLIGHTLY SOUR, SOFT.

HISTORY:

Staffordshire oatcakes are the main representatives of batter pancakes
made in the southern Pennines and North Midlands. This area has a
long tradition of oatcake making. Murray (c. 1974) cites reports of
oatcakes and oatbread from the late eighteenth century in
Staffordshire and Derbyshire. The batter was apparently mixed in a
tub kept especially for the purpose, giving the cakes a sour flavour. In
1813, Sir Humphry Davy observed, 'The Derbyshire miners in winter
prefer oatcakes to wheaten bread; finding that this kind of
nourishment enables them to support their strength and perform their
labour better.' The people of the Staffordshire pottery towns have kept
the habit of eating thick oatmeal pancakes. The tradition flourishes
and many oatcake makers are working in the area. Derbyshire oatcakes
are similar but almost extinct.

TECHNIQUE:

The recipes used by professional oatcake makers are kept secret. This
is a domestic recipe: equal quantities of flour and fine oatmeal are
mixed with salt, water, yeast and a little melted bacon fat. It is left to
ferment for about 30 minutes, poured in small amounts on a hot
griddle and allowed to cook until bubbles appear on the surface, then
turned to cook the other side.

REGION OF PRODUCTION:

NORTH MIDLANDS, STAFFORDSHIRE.

Toffee Apples

DESCRIPTION:

A WHOLE FRESH APPLE DIPPED IN HIGH-BOILED SUGAR SYRUP, 130–150G WEIGHT. COLOUR: DEEP, BRIGHT CHERRY RED WITH A LITTLE OF THE NATURAL APPLE COLOUR SHOWING WHERE THE SUGAR HAS COATED INCOMPLETELY. FLAVOUR: SWEET SUGAR, TART APPLE. COMPOSITION: APPLES, SUGAR, CREAM OF TARTAR, COLOURING.

HISTORY:

The earliest recorded allusion to toffee apples dates from early last century. However, the use of the term as soldiers' slang for a type of bomb used in the First World War suggests that they were well known and probably have a much longer history than that. The apparent use of the word 'toffee' in a specialized sugar-boilers' sense (i.e. to mean simple boiled sugar as opposed to the mixture of sugar and dairy produce which this word denotes in common English) may also indicate an older origin. Possibly toffee apples were a crude, more widespread version of the Norfolk Biffin, described by Mary Norwak as a dried apple of the Beefing variety, crusted with melted sugar. Biffins seem to have disappeared, but ordinary toffee apples are easily available for a few weeks in the autumn. There is a strong association with funfairs. They were once made on a small scale by showmen at fairgrounds, but this habit appears to have died. One company now seems to supply the market from a base at Solihull in the Midlands, coincidentally the region in which many of the largest autumn fairs are held.

TECHNIQUE:

A pan of 'toffee' made from sugar and water plus a little cream of tartar or vinegar and a dash of red food colouring is boiled to hard crack (149–154°C). The apples are obtained from local farmers in the Midlands. Each apple is speared on a stick and dipped into coloured molten sugar, allowed to set and wrapped in Cellophane.

REGION OF PRODUCTION:

WEST MIDLANDS.

'I saw him even now going the way of all flesh, that is to say towards the kitchen.'

JOHN WEBSTER, *WESTWARD HOE*

Banks's Mild

DESCRIPTION:

BANKS'S MILD IS SOLD FROM THE BARREL, IN BOTTLES AND IN CANS. IT IS A CLEAR COPPER BROWN WITH A CREAM HEAD. MILD IS GENERALLY LIGHTLY FLAVOURED, SLIGHTLY SWEET, WITH A WINY NOTE. THE HOPS ARE NOT SO PRONOUNCED AS IN BITTER, HENCE THE NAME. IT IS ABOUT 3.5 PER CENT ALCOHOL BY VOLUME.

HISTORY:

Mild originally denoted beer that was neither acid nor stale; later it came to mean one that was mildly hopped. Dark milds may have developed from the porters which were well known in parts of England (Jackson, 1993). Mild was used at harvest as a long drink for field workers; it retained identity as a thirst quencher and is now associated with areas of heavy industry in the West Midlands and, to a lesser extent, Manchester. Similar beers are known as dark in Wales; a mild type made in Newcastle is called Scotch ale; and in Scotland this is called light ale or 60/- (sixty shilling) ale. The word hock, of unknown derivation, is an old name for mild in some places. Banks, a brewery in Wolverhampton which produces large quantities of mild, is owned by Wolverhampton and Dudley Breweries, founded in 1890. At least a dozen other brewers market milds.

TECHNIQUE:

Banks prepares its own malt from Maris Otter barley, grown by specified farms, and has its own borehole for water. The wort is strained off into a brew kettle and boiled with a mixture of hop varieties, including Goldings (from Kent), Fuggles (from

Worcestershire), Progress and Bramling Cross, for 60–90 minutes. The wort is strained and cooled and yeast added. Fermentation lasts about 7 days after which the beer is fined with leaf isinglass, primed and put in casks (95 per cent of the total production), or pasteurized for bottling and canning.

REGION OF PRODUCTION:
WEST MIDLANDS.

Bitter Beer (Burton-Upon-Trent): Marston's Pedigree

DESCRIPTION:
THE COLOUR IS BRIGHT COPPER-GOLD; THE FLAVOUR SHARP, FRUITY WITH A SULPHURY NOTE; LIGHT-BODIED. PEDIGREE IS 4.5 PER CENT ALCOHOL BY VOLUME.

HISTORY:
The main factor in the development of a particular beer style is the water supply. Here, it is rich in gypsum. A tradition of brewing on a large scale has existed in the town since at least the thirteenth century. Wilson (1973) notes that Burton ale was being sold in London by 1630. The town has given its name to a process called 'burtonizing', i.e. adding mineral salts to water to give a beer similar to that of Burton.

Marston's Pedigree is an example of the type of beer known as bitter. It is distinguished by its employment of the 'Burton Union' system, a method which was fully developed by the early nineteenth century. It is based on a complex, linked series of casks and troughs through which the fermenting beer flows. It has been in use so long that strains of yeast unique to the system have developed. Jackson (1993) considers the process may have originated from a habit of catching the overflow from casks which fermented too vigorously. Two of the largest brewers in Burton abandoned the method as too cumbersome and costly; it is now unique to Marston's, who have been brewing for almost 100 years. Bass Charrington use yeast derived from the Union system in some of their beers.

The expressions 'pale ale' and 'bitter' are not well defined and overlap to some extent. Pale ale is the older, used in the 1800s to distinguish newly fashionable, light beers from older, darker brews; the word bitter came into common use around the time of World War II. Many people associate pale ale with bottled beer and bitter with draught.

TECHNIQUE:

Brewing begins with a mash of crushed pale ale malt mixed with liquor (water) at about 70°C for several hours; the wort (liquid) is strained off into a brew kettle and boiled with Fuggles and Goldings hops for 60–90 minutes; the mixture is strained and cooled and the yeast favoured by Marston's is added. All the yeast used in the brewery is derived from the Union system, which has evolved to give a powdery strain that remains in suspension. Fermentation begins in open square tanks. With Union fermentation, after 2 days the wort is dropped to the sets of unions below; it first arrives in a long trough whence it is fed by pipe into casks below; it returns from cask to trough via swan-neck pipes, and then feeds back into the cask. This circulation continues for 3–4 days. The brewery has the capacity to produce about 40 per cent of their beer by the Union system. It is racked into conventional casks to stand for 3–4 days before distribution. If it is to be bottled, it is first filtered and pasteurized.

REGION OF PRODUCTION:

MIDLANDS, BURTON-UPON-TRENT (STAFFORDSHIRE).

Cider Brandy

DESCRIPTION:

THIS IS A PALE STRAW YELLOW; IT HAS A PRONOUNCED APPLE BOUQUET AND IS RICH AND SPICY ON THE PALATE. IT IS 42 PER CENT ALCOHOL BY VOLUME.

HISTORY:

Cider spirits were being distilled in England by the second half of the seventeenth century, and royal cider, which was cider fortified with cider brandy, was also made at this time. During the eighteenth century, the local spirit was eclipsed by imported brandy (for the rich) and home-produced gin (for the poor). The tradition of distilling almost vanished. Both the companies now involved cite evidence for its continuance but it is extremely difficult to find documentation, as it was illegal and covert. The first licence granted by Customs & Excise for distillation of cider brandy in this country went to the King Offa Distillery at Hereford Cider Museum in the early 1980s. Since then, one other has been granted, to the Somerset Cider Brandy Company, Kingsbury Episcopi. Cider brandy is also blended with either apple juice or cider to make aperitifs, liqueurs and a product similar to the royal cider referred to above.

TECHNIQUE:

Somerset Royal Cider Brandy comes from apples grown by the company on their own land. They are picked and pressed late in the year, the juice fermented in December and January, the spirit distilled January–May. Ageing is still subject to experiment; barrels from various sources are used.

Hereford Cider Brandy is distilled slowly, twice, in a small copper pot still. The spirit is matured for 5 years in casks of English oak.

REGION OF PRODUCTION:

WEST MIDLANDS; SOUTH WEST ENGLAND.

Indian Pale Ales (I.P.A.): Worthington White Shield

DESCRIPTION:

WHITE SHIELD IS SOLD IN BOTTLES; ITS COLOUR IS LIGHT, BRIGHT COPPER-GOLD. THE FLAVOUR IS DRY, WITH MARKED BITTERNESS. IT IS CHARACTERIZED BY A HIGHER ORIGINAL GRAVITY THAN MANY ORDINARY ALES AND BITTERS, BEING 5.6 PER CENT ALCOHOL BY VOLUME. WHITE SHIELD IS ONE OF FEW BEERS PRODUCED IN BRITAIN TO UNDERGO SECONDARY FERMENTATION IN THE BOTTLE. IPAS IN GENERAL ARE STRONGLY HOPPED, WITH FLOWERY AROMAS. BECAUSE OF THE SECONDARY FERMENTATION, THERE IS A YEAST SEDIMENT.

HISTORY:

In the nineteenth century, Burton-upon-Trent, already an important centre of brewing, had good links by river and canal to sea-ports, allowing transport of such heavy and fragile cargo as bottled beer. The beer in the local style, known as pale ale, was exported to various parts of the British Empire, including India. A particular type evolved for this market, distinguished by a high original gravity (which allowed for a secondary fermentation in the bottle during the voyage) and a heavy flavouring of hops, which acted as a preservative protecting the beer from infection by wild yeasts. 2–2.5kg of hops per barrel (about 80 litres) was typical (Jackson, 1993). The style became popular in Britain, although modern IPAs have a lower gravity and are less heavily hopped. Few are now bottle-conditioned. There has been a new interest in IPAs, with several breweries reviving them.

White Shield was originally brewed by Worthington in Burton. This company was founded in the mid-eighteenth century and remained independent until acquisition by Bass in 1927. The original brewery was closed in the 1960s, but Bass still produces White Shield.

TECHNIQUE:

A conventional British brewing process is followed. Northdown and Challenger hops are added and Bass yeast used. After fermentation, the beer is filtered, primed with sucrose and a different yeast strain and bottled. It is warm-conditioned for 2–3 weeks, then released on the market. Ideally, it is stored for 6–18 months in a cool cellar while flavour develops further.

REGION OF PRODUCTION:

EAST MIDLANDS, BURTON-UPON-TRENT (STAFFORDSHIRE).

Perry

DESCRIPTION:

THE FERMENTED DRINK FROM THE JUICE OF PEARS IS PALE STRAW-GOLD. THE FLAVOUR OF FARM-MADE PERRIES IS VARIABLE; THEY MAY BE FERMENTED TO DRYNESS, BUT WILL RETAIN A DISTINCT PEAR BOUQUET. THEY ARE 6–8 PER CENT ALCOHOL BY VOLUME.

HISTORY:

It is probable that few people know much about perry although most are almost certainly aware of its most famous manifestation, Babycham. Yet perry has been made in southern England for centuries. The name originally applied to wild pear trees, and later was transferred to the drink produced from their fruit. As with cider and cider apples, particular varieties of pear are grown expressly for making perry.

Less attention has been paid to the history of perry than of cider. It seems to have been less well known outside its native region. That said, there are many references to production in Worcestershire and other Western counties in the medieval and early modern periods (Davies, 1993) and it shared in cider's popularity and esteem during the seventeenth century. It was even, said the poet Southey, sold in Georgian London as champagne. However, the fame did not last. By the end of the nineteenth century, *Law's Grocer's Manual* observed that it was chiefly prepared in the counties of Devon, Gloucester, Hereford and Worcester, that it was still popular in those districts, but that 'elsewhere it seems to have declined in public favour'. At this time the best perry was quite strong, about 9 per cent alcohol and sometimes bottled by the Champagne method.

The drink might have remained as obscure as the word had it not been for developments shortly after World War II. An especially good sparkling perry was exhibited at local agricultural shows by the Showering family of Shepton Mallet, Somerset. It won many prizes and was nicknamed 'baby champion' or 'baby-champ', later contracted to the brand name Babycham. The fact that perry did not have a clear place in the hierarchy of drinks worked to its advantage: 'clever use of a brand name, coupled with a reminder of the drink's claim to be a wine, brilliantly did the rest' (Dunkling, 1992). Gloucester, Herefordshire and Worcestershire perry have all been awarded Protected Geographical Indication (PGI).

TECHNIQUE:

The method for producing perry is essentially the same as that for cider. The fruit is harvested, milled to a pulp and pressed to extract the juice, which is treated with sulphur dioxide and fermented. The difference lies in the treatment towards the end of fermentation. Much perry is bottled and allowed to undergo a secondary fermentation to give a sparkling drink. Commercially, the carbonation is required to be uniform and a little carbon dioxide may be added to ensure the correct level of 'sparkle'.

REGION OF PRODUCTION:

WEST MIDLANDS; SOUTH WEST ENGLAND.

Worcestershire Sauce

DESCRIPTION:

OPAQUE, DARK BROWN COLOUR, WITH A SWEET-SOUR TASTE INFUSED WITH AROMATICS AND PEPPERY SPICES.

HISTORY:

Lea & Perrins Original and Genuine Worcestershire Sauce is a trademark and each bottle bears a characteristic orange label. It is one of the longest-lived and most celebrated store sauces, admired and appreciated by British cooks and diners. On the one hand it imparts taste and flavour to a cookery that may have lacked those qualities, on the other it imparts zest and strong taste to palates that need them.

The recipe is said (by Lea & Perrins Ltd) to have been brought to Britain from India by Marcus, Lord Sandys. In 1835 he commissioned a Worcester pharmacy owned by John Lea and William Perrins to make it up. The mixture was considered inedible and the jars were placed on one side and forgotten. On their rediscovery a year or so later, the sauce was tasted and discovered to have matured, with a very beneficial effect on flavour. The company bought the recipe from Lord Sandys and the sauce was first manufactured and sold in 1837. It was being advertised by 1843 in the *Naval and Military Gazette* as 'Lea & Perrin's Worcestershire Sauce, prepared from a recipe of a nobleman in that county'.

TECHNIQUE:

The precise recipe and process are trade secrets. Raw materials are vinegar, molasses, sugar, salt, tamarinds, shallots, garlic and unspecified spices and flavourings. The vegetables are matured in vinegar, and the anchovies in brine for 3 years. The ingredients are mixed together and infused for 3 months. The mixture is filtered, other ingredients are added and the sauce is bottled.

'Original and genuine' Worcestershire sauce is unique to one company, Lea & Perrins Ltd, whose market share is 98.2 per cent; 55 per cent of this is exported. Several other firms produce similar sauces under the name Worcester or Worcestershire.

REGION OF PRODUCTION:

WEST MIDLANDS.

The Midlands and East Anglia

Address Book

Trade Associations and Interest Groups

Asparagus Growers Associaton www.british-asparagus.co.uk
Association of Master Bakers www.masterbakers.co.uk
Association of Scottish Shellfish Growers www.assg.co.uk
Bee Farmers Association www.beefarmers.co.uk
Biscuit, Cake, Chocolate and Confectionary Alliance www.bcca.org.
Bramley Apple Information Service www.bramleyapples.co.uk
Bee Keepers Association www.bbka.org.uk
British Carrot Growers Association www.bcga.info
British Cheese Board www.cheeseboard.co.uk
British Deer Farmers Association www.bdfa.co.uk
British Goose Producers Association www.goose.cc
British Herb Trade Association www.bhta.org.uk
British Pig Association www.britishpigs.co.uk
British Summer Fruits www.britishsummerfruits.co.uk
British Soft Drinks Association www.britishsoftdrinks.com
British Waterfowl Association www.waterfowl.org.uk
Brogdale Horticultural Trust www.brogdale.org
Campaign for Real Ale www.camra.org.uk
Carrot Growers Association www.bcga.info

COMMON GROUND www.england-in-particular.info
CURRY CLUB www.thecurryclub.org.uk
DAIRY TRADE FEDERATION www.dairyuk.org
ENGLISH APPLES AND PEARS www.englishapplesandpears.co.uk
ENGLISH FARM CIDER CENTRE www.middlefarm.com
FOOD FROM BRITAIN www.foodfrombritain.co.uk
FOOD AND DRINK FEDERATION www.fdf.org.uk
GAME CONSERVANCY TRUST www.gct.org.uk
GIN AND VODKA ASSOCIATION OF GREAT BRITAIN
www.ginvodka.org
GUILD OF Q BUTCHERS www.guildofqbutchers.com
HENRY DOUBLEDAY RESEARCH ASSOCIATION
(ORGANIC GARDENING AND FOOD) www.gardenorganic.org.uk
HERB SOCIETY www.herbsociety.co.uk
KENTISH COBNUTS ASSOCIATION
www.kentishcobnutsassciation.co.uk
MEAT AND LIVESTOCK COMMISSION www.mlc.org.uk
NATIONAL FRUIT COLLECTION www.webvalley.co.uk
NATIONAL ASSOCIATION OF CIDER MAKERS www.cideruk.com
NATIONAL FARMERS UNION www.nfuonline.com
NATIONAL FEDERATION OF WOMEN'S INSTITUTES
www.womens-institute.co.uk
NATIONAL MARKET TRADERS FEDERATION www.nmtf.co.uk
NATIONAL SHEEP ASSOCIATION www.nationalsheep.org.uk
QUALITY MEAT SCOTLAND www.qmscotland.co.uk
RARE BREEDS SURVIVAL TRUST www.rbst.org.uk
SAUSAGE APPRECIATION SOCIETY www.sausagefans.com
SCOTCH MALT WHISKY SOCIETY www.smws.com
SCOTTISH ASSOCIATION OF MASTER BAKERS www.samb.co.uk
SCOTTISH ASSOCIATION OF MEAT WHOLESALERS
www.scottish-meat-wholesalers.org.uk
SCOTTISH CROP RESEARCH INSTITUTE www.scri.sari.ac.uk

SCOTTISH FEDERATION OF MEAT TRADERS ASSOCIATION
www.sfmta.co.uk

SCOTTISH QUALITY SALMON www.scottishsalmon.co.uk

SEA FISH INDUSTRY AUTHORITY www.seafish.org.uk

SEASONING AND SPICE ASSOCIATION (UK)
www.seasoningandspice.org.uk

SHELLFISH ASSOCIATION OF GREAT BRITAIN www.shellfish.org.uk

SOIL ASSOCIATION www.soilassociation.org

SOUTH-WEST OF ENGLAND CIDER MAKERS ASSOCIATION
http://tinyurl.com/pylmg

SPECIALIST CHEESEMAKERS ASSOCIATION
www.specialistcheesemakers.co.uk

TASTE OF SHROPSHIRE www.shropshiretourism.info/food-and-drink/

TASTE OF THE WEST www.tasteofthewest.co.uk

TASTE OF WALES LTD www.wela.co.uk

TASTES OF ANGLIA LTD www.tastesofanglia.com

THREE COUNTIES CIDER AND PERRY ASSOCIATION
www.thethreecountiesciderandperryassociation.co.uk

TRADITIONAL FARM FRESH TURKEY ASSOCIATION
www.golden-promise.co.uk

UK TEA COUNCIL www.teacouncil.co.uk

UNITED KINGDOM VINEYARDS ASSOCIATION
www.englishwineproducers.com

WATERCRESS GROWERS ASSOCIATION www.watercress.co.uk

WINE AND SPIRIT TRADE ASSOCIATION www.wsta.co.uk

PRODUCERS, SUPPLIERS AND PARTICULAR INTEREST GROUPS

This is by no means an exhaustive list, but this list will point readers wishing to sample a taste of Britain in the right direction. Where possible, a website is given. For smaller organizations or individuals without a functioning website, a postal address is given.

The address book echoes the structure of the text, organized into categories that roughly reflect the natural order of a visit to market: fruit and vegetables, dairy, fishmonger, butchery, bakery, confectioners, drinks and condiments.

Fruit

BLACK WORCESTER PEAR

Countryside and Conservation Section, Environmental Services Department, Hereford & Worcester County Council
www.worcestershire.gov.uk
The English Fruit Co, River House, Stour Street,
Canterbury CT1 2PA.

CARELESS GOOSEBERRY

Mr Preston, Egton Bridge Old Gooseberry Society, 10 St Johns Croft, Wakefeld, WF1 2QR.
G. Cragg, The Gooseberry Association Show, The Crown Pub, Lower Peover, Cheshire

Vegetables

SEAKALE

Michael Paske Farms Ltd, The Estate Office, Honington, Grantham, Lincolnshire NG32 2PG.

Dairy Produce

Cheese

Derby cheese
Fowler's of Earlswood www.traditionalcheeses.co.uk

Stilton cheese
Olive Middleton, The Stilton Cheesemakers Association, PO Box 11, Buxton, Derby SK17 6DD.

Hereford Hops cheese
Malvern Cheesewrights, Manor house, Malvern Road, Lower Wick, Worcester WR2 4BS.

Fish & Seafood

Cockle (Stiffkey Blues)
The North Norfolk Fisherman's Association, 104 Overstrand Road, Cromer, Norfolk.

Cromer crab
R. & J. Davies, 7 Garden Street, Cromer, Norfolk NR7 9HN.

Mussel
Eastern Sea Fisheries Joint Committee www.esfjc.co.uk
Brancaster Staithe Fisherman's Society, The Retreat, King's Lynn, Norfolk PE31 8BX.

Potted crab
The North Norfolk Shellfisherman's Association, 104 Overstrand Road, Cromer, Norfolk.

Red herring
H.S. Fishing Ltd, Sutton Road, Great Yarmouth NR30 3NA.

Smoked sprat
Butley Orford Oysterage www.butleyorfordoysterage.co.uk

Yarmouth bloater
The Lowestoft Laboratory, Centre for Environment, Fisheries and Aquaculture Science www.cefas.co.uk

Meat

CATTLE

LINCOLN RED CATTLE

The Lincoln Red Cattle Society www.lincolnredcattlesociety.co.uk

OLD HORNED HEREFORD CATTLE

The Hereford Cattle Society www.herefordcattle.org

Lower Hurst Farm www.lowerhurstfarm.co.uk

James Wickens Butchers, Castle Street, Winchelsea, Nr Rye,
East Sussex TN36 4HU.

PIGS

TAMWORTH PIG

Chesterton Farm Shop www.chestertonfarm.freeserve.co.uk

Tamworth Pig Breeders' Club www.tamworthbreedersclub.co.uk

Meat Products

FIDGET PIE

R. & J. Lodge, Greens End Road, Meltham, Hudders?eld,
Yorkshire HD7 3NW.

LINCOLNSHIRE SAUSAGE

A.W. Curtis & Sons Ltd, Long Leys Road, Lincoln,
Lincolnshire LN1 1DX.

MELTON MOWBRAY PORK PIE

Dickinson & Morris www.porkpie.co.uk

NEWMARKET SAUSAGES

Musk's www.musks.com

Powter's www.powters.co.uk

PRESSED TONGUE (SUFFOLK CURE)

Emmett's Stores www.emmettsham.co.uk

REESTIT MUTTON

Globe Butchers, Lerwick, Shetland www.globebutchers.co.uk

SPICED BEEF Heal Farm www.healfarm.co.uk

Suffolk ham

Emmett's Stores www.emmettsham.co.uk

F.E. Neave and Son www.feneave.co.uk

Rolfe's of Walsham, The High Street, Walsham-le-Willows, Nr
Bury-St-Edmunds, Suffolk IP31 3AZ.

Suffolk sweet-cured bacon

Emmett's Stores www.emmettsham.co.uk

F.E. Neave and Son www.feneave.co.uk

Rolfe's of Walsham, The High Street, Walsham-le-Willows, Nr
Bury-St-Edmunds, Suffolk IP31 3AZ.

Griddle-breads, biscuits & Puddings

Ashbourne gingerbread

Spencers Original Ashbourne Gingerbread, William Spencer & Son,
37/39 Market Place, Ashbourne, Derbyshire DE6 1EU.

Market Drayton gingerbread

The Gingerbread Sanctuary, Pell Wall House, Market Drayton,
Shropshire TF9 2AB.

Cakes & Pies

Bakewell pudding

The Old Original Bakewell Pudding
Shopwww.bakewellspuddingshop.co.uk

The Bakewell Pudding Parlour, Water Street, Bakewell DE14EW.

Bloomer's Original Bakewell Puddings, Water Street, Water Lane,
Bakewell, Berbushire DE45 2LX.

Melton Hunt cake

Ye Olde Pork Pie Shoppe www.porkpie.co.uk

Norfolk Knobs

Merv's Hot Bread Kitchen, 38 Market Place, Wymondham,
Norfolk NR17 0AX.

Confectionery

TOFFEE APPLES
Evan's Toffee Apples www.evanstoffeeapples.co.uk

Aromatics & Condiments

CIDER VINEGAR
C. Collins, The Cyder House, Aspall Hall, Stowmarket, Suffolk
IP14 6PD.

MERRYDOWN
www.merrydown.co.uk
Franklin's Cider Farm, The Cliffs, Little Hereford, Ludlow,
Shropshire S78 4LW.

COLMAN'S MUSTARD
Colmans of Norwich www.colmansmustardshop.com
Colman's Mustard Museum, 3 Bridewell Alley, Norwich.

MALDON SEA SALT
The Maldon Crystal Salt Co Ltd www.maldonsalt.co.uk

MARMITE
Unilever www.marmite.com

MEDLAR JELLY
Stonham Hedgerow Products www.stonhamhedgerow.co.uk
Garden of Suffolk Preserves, 119 Plumstead Road,
Norwich NR1 4JT.
Melanie Knibbs, St Nicholas, Bevis Way, King's Lynn,
Norfolk PE30 3AG.
Elsenham Quality Foods, Bishop's Stortford, Hertfordshire,
CM22 6DT.
Wilkin and Sons Ltd, Tiptree www.tiptree.com

SEA LAVENDER HONEY
Margaret Thomas, 25 Tyrone Road, Southend-on-Sea, Essex SS1 3HE

Beverages

Bitter beer (Burton-upon-Trent)

Marston's Beer www.marstonsdontcompromise.co.uk

Cider brandy

The Hereford Cider Museum www.cidermuseum.co.uk

The Somerset Distillery www.ciderbrandy.co.uk

Cider (Eastern tradition)

John Hallam, 27 Fraser Street, Windmill Hill, Bedminster, Bristol
BS3 4LZ.

Old ale

Greene King www.abbotale.co.uk

PGOs and PGIs

Britain and continental Europe possess an enormous range of
wonderful food. When a product's reputation extends beyond national
borders, however, it can find itself in competition with products using
the same name and passing themselves off as genuine. This unfair
competition discourages producers and misleads consumers, and for
this reason the European Union in 1992 created systems known as
Protected Designation of Origin and Protected Geographical
Indication to promote and protect regionally important food products.
A Protected Designation of Origin (PDO) describes a food that is
produced, processed and prepared in a given geographical area, using a
recognised skill. A Protected Geographical Indication (PGI)
demonstrates a geographical link between a foodstuff and a specific region
in at least one of the stages of production, processing or preparation.

For more information, visit

http://ec.europa.eu/agriculture/qual/en/uk_en.htm

Bibliography

Unless otherwise indicated, the place of publication is London and the country of publication is the United Kingdom.

Acton, Eliza (1845), *Modern Cookery for Private Families*, facsimile ed., introduction by Elizabeth Ray, 1993, Southover Press, Lewes.

Ayrton, Elizabeth (1975), *The Cookery of England*, André Deutsch.

——— (1980), *English Provincial Cooking*, Mitchell Beazley.

Beeton, Isabella (1861), *Beeton's Book of Household Management*, facsimile ed. 1982, Chancellor Press.

Black, M. (1989), *Paxton and Whitfeld's Fine Cheese*, Little Brown.

Boyd, Lizzie (1976), *British Cookery*, Croom Helm, Bromley.

Bradley, Richard (1736), *The Country Housewife and Lady's Director*, ed. Caroline Davidson, 1982, Prospect Books.

Bradley, Martha (1756), *The British Housewife*, facsimile ed. 1997-8, Prospect Books, Totnes.

Burdett, O. (1935), *A Little Book of Cheese*, Gerald Howe Ltd.

Cassell's (1896), *Cassell's Dictionary of Cookery* (First ed. c. 1875).

Castelvetro, Giacomo (1989), *The Fruit, Herbs & Vegetables of Italy*, translated and edited by Gillian Riley from the manuscript of 1614, Viking.

Cutting, C.L. (1955), *Fish Saving, A History of Fish Processing from Ancient to Modern Times*, Hill.

David, Elizabeth (1968), *English Potted Meats and Fish Pastes*, reprinted in *An Omelette and a Glass of Wine*, (1984), Robert Hale.

——— (1970), *Spices, Salt and Aromatics in the English Kitchen*, Penguin Books.

——— (1977), *English Bread and Yeast Cookery*, Allen Lane.

——— (1992), 'Anglo-American Tomato Ketchup', Petits Propos Culinaires 40.

Davidson, Alan E. (1979) *North Atlantic Seafood*, Macmillan.

——— (1988) *Seafood, A Connoisseur's Guide and Cookbook*, Mitchell Beazley.

——— (1991), *Fruit*, Mitchell Beazley.

——— (1993) 'Sherbets', *Liquid Nourishment*, ed. C.A. Wilson, Edinburgh University Press.

Davies, S. (1993), 'Vinetum Britannicum, Cider and Perry in the seventeenth century', *Liquid Nourishment*, ed. C.A. Wilson, Edinburgh University Press.

Defoe, Daniel (1724–6), *A Tour Through the Whole Island of Great Britain*, Penguin ed. 1971.

Dunkling, L. (1992), *The Guinness Drinking Companion*, Guinness Publishing, Enfield.

Dyson, John (1977), *Business in Great Waters*, Angus and Robertson.

Elsenham Quality Foods Ltd (n.d.), Patum Peperium, a brief history, Bishop's Stortford.

Evelyn, John (1699), *Acetaria. A Discourse of Sallets*, new edition, 1996, Prospect Books, Totnes.

Festing, S. (1977), *Fishermen, a community living from the sea*, David and Charles, Newton Abbot.

Finney, Thomas B. (1915), *Handy Guide for Pork Butchers*, Finney & Co, Manchester.

Glasse, Hannah (1747), *The Art of Cookery Made Plain and Easy*, facsimile 1983, Prospect Books.

———— (1772), *The Compleat Confectioner*.

Grigson, Jane (1971), *Good Things*, Michael Joseph.

———— (1974), *English Food*, Macmillan.

———— (1975), *Fish Cookery*, Penguin Books.

———— (1982), *Fruit*, Michael Joseph.

———— (1984), *Observer Guide to British Cookery*, Michael Joseph.

Hagen, Ann (1995), *A Second Handbook of Anglo-Saxon Food & Drink*. Production and Distribution, Anglo-Saxon Books, Hockwold cum Wilton.

Hartley, Dorothy (1954), *Food in England*, Macdonald and Janes.

Hodgson, W.C. (1957), *The Herring and Its Fishery*, Routledge and Kegan Paul.

Howes, F.N. (1979), *Plants and Beekeeping*, Faber and Faber.

Hughes, Edward (1952), *North Country Life in the Eighteenth Century, The North East 1700–1750*, Oxford University Press.

Jackson, Michael (1989), *Malt Whisky Companion*, Dorling Kindersley.

———— (1993), *Michael Jackson's Beer Companion*, Mitchell Beazley.

Kitchiner, W. (1817), *The Cook's Oracle* (1829 ed.). Larousse Gastronomique (1938), Paris.

Lloyd, L.C. and A.J. (1931), *Shrewsbury Cakes, the story of a famous delicacy*.

Mabey, David (1978), *In Search of Food, traditional eating and drinking in Britain*, Macdonald and Jane's.

MacCarthy, D. (1989), *Food Focus 1*, Food From Britain.

MacClure, Victor (1955), *Good Appetite, My Companion*, Odhams.

McNeill, F.M. (1929), *The Scots Kitchen*, Blackie, Glasgow.

———— (1946), *Recipes from Scotland*, Albyn, Edinburgh.

———— (1956), *The Scots Cellar*, Lochar, Moffat (1992).

———— (1963), *The Scots Kitchen* (2nd ed.), Blackie, Glasgow.

Markham, Gervase (1615), *The English Hus-wife*.

Mayhew, Henry (1861), *London Labour and the London Poor*.

Morgan, Joan and Richards, Alison (1993), *A Book of Apples*, Ebury Press.

Norwak, M. (1988), *A Taste of Norfolk*, Jarrold and Sons, Norwich.

Nott, J. (1726), *Cook's and Confectioner's Dictionary*, facsimile ed. 1980, Lawrence Rivington.

Raffald, E. (1769), *The Experienced English Housekeeper*, facsimile of 1782 ed. 1970, E&W Books.

Rance, Patrick (1982), *The Great British Cheese Book*, Macmillan.

Riley, Gillian (1995), 'Parsnips, now you see them-now you don't', *Disappearing Foods,* Oxford Symposium on Food and Cookery, ed. Harlan Walker, Prospect Books, Totnes.

Roach, F.A. (1985), *Cultivated Fruits of Britain*, Basil Blackwell, Oxford.

Roberts, Robert (1971), *The Classic Slum*, (Penguin Books ed., 1973).

[Rundell, Maria Eliza] (1807), *A New System of Domestic Cookery, by a Lady*.

Sala, G.A. (1859), *Twice Round the Clock*, reprint, 1971, Leicester University Press.

Samuel, S. (1860), (ed.), *The Pig*, by William Youatt.

Simon, A.L. (1960), *The Concise Encyclopaedia of Gastronomy*, Collins (1983 ed., Penguin Books).

——— (1960), *Cheeses of the World*, Faber and Faber.

Smith, Eliza (1758), *The Compleat Housewife*, first published 1727, facsimile of the 16th ed., 1983, Arlon House Publishing, Kings Langley.

Smith, J. (1989), *Fairs, Feasts and Frolics, customs and traditions in Yorkshire*, Smith Settle, Otley.

Smith, M.W.G. (1978), *A Catalogue of the Plums at the National Fruit Trials*, HMSO.

Thick, Malcolm (1998), *The Neat House Gardens*, Prospect Books, Totnes.

Tusser, Thomas (1573), *Five Hundred Points of Good Husbandry*, 1984 ed., Oxford University Press.

Vilmorin-Andrieux (1885), *The Vegetable Garden*, reprinted 1976 Jeavons-Leler, Palo Alto, USA.

White, Florence (1932), *Good Things in England*, Jonathan Cape.

Williams, R.R.(n.d.), (ed.), *Cider and Juice Apples, Growing and Processing*, University of Bristol.

Wilson, C. Anne (1973), *Food and Drink in Britain*, Constable.

——— (1985), 'I'll to Thee a Simnel Bring', Petits Propos Culinaires 19.

——— (1985), *The Book of Marmalade*, Constable.

——— (1991), (ed.), *Banquetting Stuffe*, Edinburgh University Press.

Woolgar, V.M. (1992), *Household Accounts from Medieval England*, 2 vols, The British Academy.

Wright, Joseph (1896–1905), *The English Dialect Dictionary*, Henry Frowde.

'They dined on mince, and slices of quince,
Which they ate with a runcible spoon;
And hand in hand, on the edge of the sand,
They danced by the light of the moon.'
EDWARD LEAR, 'THE OWL AND THE PUSSYCAT'

Acknowledgements

Midlands, East Midlands, East Anglia
From Norfolk Knobs to Fidget Pie
Foods from the Heart of England and East Anglia

Particular thanks to the following chefs and authors who generously contributed pieces to the book:

Delia Smith (p.14), Galton Blackiston (p.28-9), John Torode (p.57), Fergus Henderson (p.91).

The following people have kindly given the compilers information about particular foods and trades. This book could not have been completed without their assistance.

J. Adlard, Norfolk; J. Ashworth, Wymondham, Norfolk; C. Beach, King's Lynn, Norfolk; C. Bray, Herefordshire and Worcestershire County Council; G. Bulmer, Hereford; G. Cloke, Solihull, West Midlands; P.D. Davies, Lowestoft; M. Dorman, Middle Tysoe, Warwickshire; D. Eastwood, Great Yarmouth; E. Elder, Barton-on-Humber; S. Hallam, Melton Mowbray, Leicestershire; B. Harrison, Nottingham; E. Hawksley-Beesley, Stamford Bridge, Lincolnshire; N. Hodgetts, Worcester; J. Huggins, Southwold, Suffolk; N. Jerrey, Emmett's Stores, Suffolk; P. King, Kenilworth, Warwickshire; D. Myers, Horncastle, Lincolnshire; K. Neuteboom, Hemingstone, Suffolk; L. Newboult, Lincoln; D. Newton, Boston, Lincolnshire; E. Phipps, Boston, Lincolnshire; D. Powell, Ledbury, Hereford & Worcester; G. Powter, Newmarket, Suffolk; K. Pybus, Market Drayton, Shropshire; A. Sebire, Hartington, Derbyshire; Spencers, Ashbourne, Derbyshire; C. Sutherland, Brancaster, Norfolk; P. Symonds, Hereford, Hereford & Worcester; H. Watkins, Sandy, Bedfordshire; R. Westwood, Wolverhampton.